THE GRAPHIC HISTORY OF

GETTYSBURG

AMERICA'S MOST FAMOUS BATTLE AND THE TURNING POINT OF THE CIVIL WAR

Written and Illustrated by

Wayne Vansant

ZENITH PRESS

ABOUT THE AUTHOR

Writer and artist Wayne Vansant was the primary artist for Marvel's *The 'Nam* for more than five years. Since then he has written and or illustrated many historically accurate graphic histories such as *Antietam: The Fiery Trial* (with the National Park Service) and *The Vietnam War: A Graphic History.* He recently published *Normandy* (Zenith, 2012), which examines D-Day from the Allied perspective, and is currently working on a graphic history of the Battle of the Bulge.

First published in 2013 by MBI Publishing Company and Zenith Press, an imprint of MBI Publishing Company, 400 First Avenue North, Suite 300, Minneapolis, MN 55401 USA

© 2013 Zenith Press
Text and illustrations © 2013 Wayne Vansant

Zenith Press titles are also available at discounts in bulk quantity for industrial or sales-promotional use. For details write to Special Sales Manager at MBI Publishing Company, 400 First Avenue North, Suite 300, Minneapolis, MN 55401 USA.

To find out more about our books, visit us online at www.zenithpress.com.

ISBN-13: 978-0-7603-4406-4

All photographs are from the author's collection unless noted otherwise.

Editor: Erik Gilg
Design Manager: James Kegley
Design: Wayne Vansant
Layout: Chris Fayers

Printed in China

CONTENTS

Army of the Potomac at the Battle of Gettysburg

State	Engaged Strength	Infantry Regiments	Cavalry Regiments	Artillery Batteries
Connecticut	1,268	5	–	1
Delaware	485	2	–	–
Illinois	1,021	1	2	–
Indiana	2,035	5	1	–
Maine	3,752	10	1	3
Maryland	1,953	3	2	1
Massachusetts	6,104	19	1	4
Michigan	3,899	7	4	1
Minnesota	378	1	–	–
New Hampshire	843	3	–	1
New Jersey	4,073	12	1	2
New York	23,374	70	6	15
Ohio	4,402	13	–	4
Pennsylvania	24,067	67	8	5
Rhode Island	960	1	–	5
U.S. Regulars	7,176	13	4	22
Vermont	4,444	8	1	–
West Virginia	788	1	2	1
Wisconsin	2,155	6	–	–
Totals	**93,177**	**247**	**33**	**65**

Army of Northern Virginia at the Battle of Gettysburg

State	Engaged Strength	Infantry Regiments	Cavalry Regiments	Artillery Batteries
Alabama	5,928	17	–	2
Arkansas	429	1	–	–
Florida	739	3	–	–
Georgia	13,185	37	2	6
Louisiana	3,031	10	–	7
Maryland	981	1	1	3
Mississippi	4,929	11	1	1
North Carolina	14,182	34	2	4
South Carolina	4,959	11	2	5
Tennessee	750	3	–	–
Texas	1,250	3	–	–
Virginia	20,776	41	19	40
Totals	**71,139**	**172**	**27**	**68**

THE LONG CHANCE

FRIDAY, MAY 15, 1863—AN OMINOUS DAY FOR THE SOUTHERN CONFEDERACY. IN THE SHENANDOAH VALLEY, GEN. THOMAS J. JACKSON WAS BEING BURIED. JACKSON HAD DIED OF WOUNDS RECEIVED IN THE BATTLE OF CHANCELLORSVILLE ON MAY 2.

IRONICALLY, JACKSON WAS NOT WOUNDED BY ENEMY FIRE, BUT BY HIS OWN MEN MISTAKING HIM AND HIS STAFF AS UNION CAVALRY IN THE DARKNESS.

ON THE DAY OF JACKSON'S FUNERAL, GEN. ROBERT E. LEE, COMMANDER OF THE ARMY OF NORTHERN VIRGINIA, WAS SUMMONED TO MEET WITH CONFEDERATE PRESIDENT JEFFERSON DAVIS AND HIS CABINET IN RICHMOND, THE CONFEDERATE CAPITAL.

THE WAR HAD GONE WELL FOR THE CONFEDERACY IN THE PAST 6 MONTHS, BUT EVENTS WERE UNFOLDING ON THE MISSISSIPPI RIVER THAT COULD LEAD TO DISASTER ...

... LEE HAD BEEN SUMMONED TO RICHMOND TO GIVE ADVICE AND POSSIBLY FORCES TO RELIEVE THE CONFEDERATE GARRISON AT VICKSBURG.

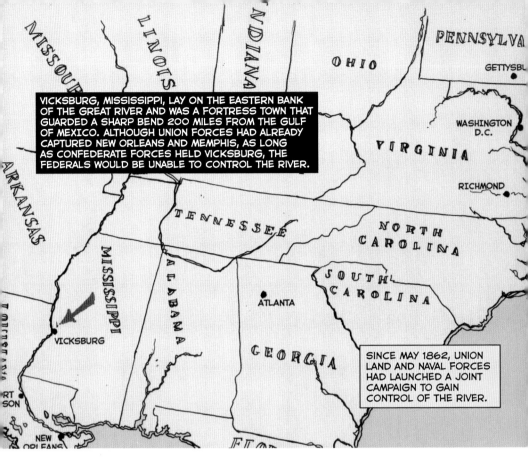

VICKSBURG, MISSISSIPPI, LAY ON THE EASTERN BANK OF THE GREAT RIVER AND WAS A FORTRESS TOWN THAT GUARDED A SHARP BEND 200 MILES FROM THE GULF OF MEXICO. ALTHOUGH UNION FORCES HAD ALREADY CAPTURED NEW ORLEANS AND MEMPHIS, AS LONG AS CONFEDERATE FORCES HELD VICKSBURG, THE FEDERALS WOULD BE UNABLE TO CONTROL THE RIVER.

SINCE MAY 1862, UNION LAND AND NAVAL FORCES HAD LAUNCHED A JOINT CAMPAIGN TO GAIN CONTROL OF THE RIVER.

IN APRIL 1863, FORCES UNDER THE COMMAND OF GEN. ULYSSES S. GRANT CROSSED THE RIVER SOUTH OF VICKSBURG AND BEGAN A FIGHTING MARCH TOWARD THE BELEAGUERED CITY FROM ITS SCANTLY GUARDED REAR.

KNOWING THE FALL OF VICKSBURG WOULD CUT THE CONFEDERACY IN 2, DAVIS WANTED TO CONVINCE LEE TO SEND PART OF HIS ARMY TO MISSISSIPPI TO BOLSTER THE DEFENSE OF VICKSBURG.

LEE WAS AGAINST THIS PLAN, AND HE PRESENTED A CONVINCING ARGUMENT.

LEE ARGUED THAT HE SHOULD INVADE THE NORTH AGAIN AND CUT DEEP INTO PENNSYLVANIA, DRAWING THE ARMY OF THE POTOMAC INTO A DECISIVE BATTLE.

SOUTH MOUNTAIN

MARYLAND

SHARPSBURG

FREDERIC...

THIS WOULD BE LEE'S SECOND INVASION OF THE NORTH: THE FIRST HAD BEEN THE PREVIOUS SEPTEMBER, AND IT HAD ENDED BADLY. HIS REASONS NOW WERE PRETTY MUCH WHAT THEY HAD BEEN THEN.

HE KNEW THAT THE NORTHERN PEACE DEMOCRATS HAD WANTED TO END THE WAR, EVEN IF IT MEANT DISSOLUTION OF THE UNION AND CONTINUED SOUTHERN SLAVERY.

LEE'S VICTORY AT FREDERICKSBURG IN DECEMBER 1862 BROUGHT NEW CALLS FOR PRESIDENT ABRAHAM LINCOLN TO MAKE PEACE WITH THE REBELS.

PEACE NOW

I PROPOSE AN EMANCIPATION PROCLAMATION.

BUT LINCOLN, THE BRILLIANT POLITICIAN, ELEVATED THE WAR TO A HIGHER PURPOSE.

LEE'S BRILLIANT VICTORY IN MAY AT CHANCELLORSVILLE BROUGHT NEW CRIES FROM THE NORTH DEMANDING PEACE. THE UNION SOLDIERS IN THE ARMY OF THE POTOMAC WERE THEMSELVES DISPIRITED AND WEARY. A MASSACHUSETTS SERGEANT PUT IT BEST:

CALL IT WHAT YOU PLEASE, DEMORALIZATION OR DISCOURAGEMENT ...

... WE CARE NOT TO FORD RIVERS, SLEEP STANDING, AND FIGHT RUNNING, WHEN SURE DEFEAT ALWAYS AWAITS SUCH A DOOMED ARMY.

IT SEEMED THAT BOTH SIDES WERE AT AN IMPASSE.

DESPITE HIS VICTORY AT CHANCELLORSVILLE, LEE KNEW HE HAD PROBLEMS. HE KNEW THAT HE COULD NOT REMAIN ON THE DEFENSIVE FOR LONG. HE COULD NEVER MATCH THE UNION IN NUMBERS OF MEN OR IN THE INDUSTRY NEEDED TO SUPPORT THE WAR. SOONER OR LATER THE NORTHERN ARMY WOULD SIMPLY OVERWHELM HIM. AND DIVIDING HIS ARMY TO SUPPORT THE DEFENSE OF VICKSBURG WOULD JUST HASTEN THE INEVITABLE.

LEE HAD YET ANOTHER REASON TO FEEL THAT AN INVASION OF THE NORTH WAS HIS BEST OPTION. HE HAD BEEN HAVING GREAT DIFFICULTY IN PROVIDING FOOD AND CLOTHING FOR HIS ARMY AND FORAGE FOR HIS DRAFT ANIMALS. AFTER OPERATING FOR 2 YEARS IN WAR-RAVAGED VIRGINIA, THE CONFEDERATE FORCES HAD STRIPPED THE REGION OF RELIABLE PROVISIONS.

AN INVASION THROUGH PROSPEROUS, UNDISTURBED PENNSYLVANIA WOULD ALLOW HIS ARMY TO STOCKPILE SUPPLIES AND GIVE VIRGINIA TIME TO RESTORE ITSELF.

FOR 3 DAYS LEE EXPRESSED HIS PLAN TO THE CONFEDERATE CABINET: HE WOULD INVADE PENNSYLVANIA, FORCING THE ARMY OF THE POTOMAC TO PURSUE HIM THERE, AND DEFEAT THEM. PRESIDENT JEFFERSON DAVIS WAS VERY UNEASY ABOUT THE PLAN—AND POSTMASTER GENERAL JOHN REAGAN WAS BLUNTLY AGAINST IT.

FINALLY, WHAT WAS REFERRED TO AS "THE LONG CHANCE" WAS APPROVED BY THE CABINET 4 TO 1, REAGAN REFUSING TO BUDGE ON HIS DISAGREEMENT.

NOW LEE TURNED TO PREPARING HIS ARMY FOR THE MARCH NORTH. BEFORE THE LOSS OF STONEWALL JACKSON, THE ARMY OF NORTHERN VIRGINIA WAS DIVIDED INTO 2 EQUAL CORPS, 1 COMMANDED BY JACKSON AND THE OTHER BY LT. GEN. JAMES LONGSTREET. BOTH JACKSON AND LONGSTREET WERE VERY CAPABLE COMMANDERS WHOM LEE COULD RELY ON TO FULFILL THEIR TASKS WITHOUT DETAILED INSTRUCTIONS.

HOWEVER, LEE DID NOT HAVE ANOTHER COMMANDER AS STRONG AND AS TALENTED AS JACKSON, SO HE DECIDED TO DIVIDE HIS ARMY INTO NOT 2 BUT 3 CORPS.

LONGSTREET WOULD COMMAND WHAT WAS MOSTLY HIS OLD CORPS WITH THESE DIVISIONS:

RICHARD "BALDY" EWELL WOULD COMMAND THE 2ND CORPS WITH THESE DIVISIONS:

A. P. HILL WOULD COMMAND THE 3RD CORPS WITH THESE DIVISIONS:

LAFAYETTE MCLAWS

JUBAL EARLY

RICHARD ANDERSON

GEORGE PICKETT

EDWARD JOHNSON

HENRY HETH

JOHN BELL HOOD

ROBERT RODES

WILLIAM DORSEY PENDER

JAMES EWELL BROWN "JEB" STUART COMMANDED THE CAVALRY DIVISION WITH 5 BRIGADES OF HORSE CAVALRY AND 1 OF ARTILLERY.

EACH DIVISION HAD AN ARTILLERY BRIGADE NUMBERING FROM 21 TO 51 ARTILLERY PIECES. ALSO, THERE WAS AN ARTILLERY RESERVE WITH 36 PIECES.

THE MARCH NORTH

NORTH OF THE RAPPAHANNOCK RIVER, AN EVEN GREATER SHAKE-UP WAS ABOUT TO HAPPEN IN THE COMMAND STRUCTURE OF THE ARMY OF THE POTOMAC.

ON JUNE 4, 1863, OBSERVATION BALLOONS OF THE ARMY OF THE POTOMAC REPORTED THAT CONFEDERATE FORCES ACROSS THE RAPPAHANNOCK AT FREDERICKSBURG HAD ABANDONED THEIR POSITIONS.

THE ARMY COMMAND, MAJ. GEN. JOSEPH HOOKER, TELEGRAPHED PRESIDENT ABRAHAM LINCOLN THAT HE WAS PREPARING TO CROSS THE RIVER AND "PITCH IN" TO THE ENEMY.

LINCOLN SENT A MESSAGE BACK TO HOOKER THAT HE "MOST ASSUREDLY WOULD NOT." HE WANTED TO KNOW FIRST WHERE THE CONFEDERATES WERE HEADING.

LINCOLN HAD VERY LITTLE FAITH IN HOOKER, AND HE WAS, IN FACT, CONSIDERING REPLACING HIM.

HOOKER WAS JUST 1 OF A LONG LIST OF GENERALS WHO HAD FAILED TO DO LINCOLN'S BIDDING AND DEFEAT THE CONFEDERATE ARMIES IN VIRGINIA: IRVIN MCDOWELL, GEORGE B. MCCLELLAN, JOHN POPE, GEORGE B. MCCLELLAN (AGAIN), AMBROSE E. BURNSIDE, AND, FINALLY, JOE HOOKER.

HOOKER SENT OUT HIS CAVALRY TO FIND OUT WHERE LEE WAS GOING. THE CAVALRY HAD LITTLE LUCK, BECAUSE THE REBELS WERE PREPARING TO CROSS THE BLUE RIDGE MOUNTAINS INTO THE SHENANDOAH VALLEY. FROM THERE THEY WOULD MOVE NORTH INTO THE CUMBERLAND VALLEY AND INTO PENNSYLVANIA. BUT THE UNION CAVALRY DID REPORT TO HOOKER THAT THE CAVALRY CORPS OF GEN. JEB STUART HAD GATHERED NORTH OF CULPEPER COURT HOUSE AT BRANDY STATION ON THE ORANGE & ALEXANDRIA RAILROAD.

WHEN HE GOT THE NEWS, HOOKER SENT IN BRIG. GEN. ALFRED PLEASONTON'S CAVALRY CORPS.

IT WAS THERE AT BRANDY STATION ON JUNE 9, 1863, THAT THE GREATEST CAVALRY BATTLE OF THE WAR WAS FOUGHT.

BOTH SIDES SUFFERED ABOUT 1,500 CASUALTIES. THERE WAS NO CLEAR WINNER.

STUART WAS OBVIOUSLY CAUGHT BY SURPRISE AND WAS OPENLY CRITICIZED IN THE *RICHMOND EXAMINER*. ALWAYS SENSITIVE TO PUBLIC SCRUTINY, STUART WOULD TRY TO FIND A WAY TO REDEEM HIMSELF ... WITH DISASTROUS RESULTS.

FREED FROM THE BRANDY STATION BATTLE, STUART'S CAVALRY REQUIRED REST. BUT LEE WOULD NOT BE WAITING FOR HIM. HE PUT EWELL'S 2ND CORPS ON THE ROAD THE NEXT DAY WITH ORDERS TO MOVE THROUGH THE CHESTER GAP INTO THE SHENANDOAH VALLEY.

EWELL, WHO HAD LOST A LEG IN THE SECOND BATTLE OF BULL RUN, RODE ALONG WITH HIS CORPS IN A BUGGY.

BY JUNE 15, WHILE EWELL WAS FINISHING HIS TAKING OF WINCHESTER, LEE ORDERED HIS OTHER 2 CORPS TO BEGIN A QUICK MARCH NORTH. LEE WANTED HIS CAVALRY TO MOVE ALONG WITH HIS INFANTRY CORPS, BUT STUART HAD ANOTHER IDEA.

STUART ASKED PERMISSION TO HARASS HOOKER'S FORCES IN VIRGINIA, DELAYING THEIR SCREENING OF LEE'S ARMY.

LEE RELUCTANTLY AGREED, BUT MADE IT CLEAR THAT AS SOON AS THE FEDERALS CROSSED THE POTOMAC, STUART HAD TO TAKE UP A ROVING POSITION BETWEEN LEE'S ARMY AND THE ARMY OF THE POTOMAC.

AND SO THE 2 SEPARATED—LEE TO INVADE THE NORTH TO BEAT HOOKER AND STUART TO ATTEMPT SOMETHING SPECTACULAR TO REVIVE HIS REPUTATION IN THE RICHMOND PAPERS.

ON JUNE 13, HOOKER BEGAN TO MOVE HIS ARMY NORTH FROM HIS POSITION NORTH OF THE RAPPAHANNOCK AT FREDERICKSBURG. AS THE ARMY MOVED, A CONSTANT BARRAGE OF TELEGRAMS FLASHED BACK AND FORTH AMONG HOOKER, LINCOLN, AND UNION GENERAL AND CHIEF HENRY W. HALLECK. THESE MESSAGES WERE CURT, PETTY SNIPES AND CRITICISMS THAT EACH PARTY DIRECTED TOWARD THE OTHERS.

ON JUNE 24, EWELL'S CORPS CROSSED INTO PENNSYLVANIA, HIS OBJECTIVE THE STATE CAPITAL, HARRISBURG.

ON THAT SAME DAY THE CORPS OF HILL AND LONGSTREET CROSSED THE POTOMAC AT SHEPHERDSTOWN, WEST VIRGINIA, AND WILLIAMSPORT, MARYLAND. THE CONFEDERATES WERE MOVING FAST.

ON THE AFTERNOON OF JUNE 26, JUBAL EARLY'S DIVISION PASSED THROUGH THE FARMING TOWN OF GETTYSBURG. SEEING THE FRIGHTENED FACES OF THE TOWNSPEOPLE, GEN. JOHN B. GORDON PAUSED TO REASSURE THEM.

THESE TROOPS PASSED ON THROUGH GETTYSBURG, AS THEY HAD THROUGH GREENCASTLE, WAYNESBORO, AND CHAMBERSBURG. TO THEM, GETTYSBURG WAS JUST ANOTHER TOWN ON THE WAY TO VICTORY.

THE TELEGRAPHIC BICKERING AND DEBATE FROM HOOKER FINALLY CONVINCED LINCOLN AND HALLECK TO ACT. BY THE EVENING OF JUNE 27, A REPRESENTATIVE FROM THE WAR OFFICE WAS ON A TRAIN ON HIS WAY TO FREDERICK, MARYLAND.

HE WAS THERE TO INFORM HOOKER THAT HE'D BEEN RELIEVED OF COMMAND, BUT FIRST HE WENT TO THE TENT OF THE MAN WHO WAS TO REPLACE HIM.

V CORPS COMMANDER MAJ. GEN. GEORGE GORDON MEADE, 47, WAS A PENNSYLVANIA NATIVE AND WEST POINT GRADUATE. HE PROTESTED THAT THERE WERE OTHER GENERALS WHO HAD MORE SENIORITY AND WERE BETTER QUALIFIED.

WELL, I'VE BEEN TRIED AND CONDEMNED WITHOUT A HEARING...

... AND I SUPPOSE I SHALL HAVE TO GO TO THE EXECUTION.

WITH STUART OUT RIDING TO THE EAST OF THE UNION ARMY, LEE WAS STILL UNAWARE OF THE POSITION OF THE ARMY OF THE POTOMAC. BUT ON THE NIGHT OF JUNE 28, A CIVILIAN SCOUT WHO CALLED HIMSELF HARRISON WAS BROUGHT TO LEE'S TENT AT CHAMBERSBURG.

NORMALLY, LEE WOULD NOT HAVE TRUSTED THE WORD OF THIS "SPY," BUT WITH NO WORD FROM STUART, HE HAD NO CHOICE. HE SENT OUT MESSENGERS FOR THE ARMY OF NORTHERN VIRGINIA TO CONCENTRATE NEAR CASHTOWN.

HARRISON REPORTED THAT ALL 7 CORPS OF THE ARMY OF THE POTOMAC WERE ON THE NORTHERN SIDE OF THE POTOMAC.

THE ARMY OF THE POTOMAC WAS DIVIDED INTO 7 CORPS. THE CORPS AND DIVISIONS COMMANDERS WERE:

CAVALRY CORPS COMMANDER
ALFRED PLEASONTON

CAVALRY CORPS 1ST DIVISION
JOHN BUFORD

2ND DIVISION
DAVID GREGG

3RD DIVISION
JUDSON KILPATRICK

XII CORPS
HENRY W. SLOCUM

ALPHEUS WILLIAMS

JOHN W. GEARY

XI CORPS
OLIVER O. HOWARD

FRANCIS C. BARLOW

ADOLF VON STEINWEHR

CARL SCHURZ

VI CORPS
JOHN SEDGWICK

HORATIO G. WRIGHT

ALBION P. HOWE

JOHN NEWTON

V CORPS
GEORGE SYKES

JAMES BARNES

ROHEYN B. AYRES

SAMUEL W. CRAWFORD

III CORPS
DANIEL E. SICKLES

DAVID B. BIRNEY

ANDREW A. HUMPHREYS

II CORPS
WINFIELD SCOTT HANCOCK

JOHN C. CALDWELL

JOHN GIBBON

ALEXANDER HAYES

I CORPS
JOHN F. REYNOLDS

JAMES S. WADSWORTH

JOHN C. ROBINSON

ABNER DOUBLEDAY

15

SCOUTS INFORMED MEADE THAT THE TROOPS OF A. P. HILL AND LONGSTREET WERE CAMPED BETWEEN CHAMBERSBURG AND GETTYSBURG.

THE ARMY MOVED NORTH, THE CAVALRY OF BRIG. GEN. JOHN BUFORD IN THE LEAD.

ALL TROOPS MUST BE READY TO MARCH BY DAYLIGHT TOMORROW.

BUFORD'S MEN ARRIVED IN GETTYSBURG AT 11:00 AM ON THE MORNING OF JUNE 30. THE TOWNSPEOPLE WERE EXCITED, HAVING SEEN A CONFEDERATE INFANTRY BRIGADE COMING FROM THE NORTHWEST AND THEN SUDDENLY WITHDRAWING.

THAT BRIGADE WAS UNDER THE COMMAND OF JAMES JOHNSON PETTIGREW OF HENRY HETH'S DIVISION OF A. P HILL'S CORPS. SOME WOULD LATER SAY THAT THERE WAS A RUMOR OF A WAREHOUSE FULL OF SHOES IN GETTYSBURG, SOMETHING THAT THE CONFEDERATE ARMY ALWAYS NEEDED.

DIVISION COMMANDER HENRY HETH WOULD LATER CLAIM THAT HE WENT INTO GETTYSBURG THAT NEXT MORNING TO GET THOSE SHOES. HE MAY HAVE BELIEVED THAT ALL HE HAD TO FACE WAS MILITIA. SO, ALTHOUGH HE WAS WELL AWARE OF LEE'S ORDER TO AVOID A GENERAL ENGAGEMENT, HE WOULD UNWITTINGLY BEGIN THE GREATEST BATTLE OF THE WAR.

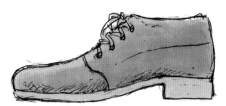

SQUARE TOED SHOES FOR BOTH FEET

THE FIRST SHOT

ON THE MORNING OF WEDNESDAY, JULY 1, 1863, LT. MARCELLUS E. JONES OF THE 8TH ILLINOIS CAVALRY SPOTTED CONFEDERATES COMING THROUGH THE MIST. THEY WERE COMING FROM THE NORTHWEST ALONG THE CHAMBERSBURG PIKE.

JONES SPOTTED A MOUNTED OFFICER 700 FEET AWAY AND FIRED A SINGLE SHOT AT HIM WITH NO RESULTS. THIS WAS THE FIRST SHOT FIRED IN THE BATTLE OF GETTYSBURG.

THEN THE CONFEDERATES FORMED A SKIRMISH LINE A MILE AND A HALF WIDE, SO JONES WITHDREW HIS PICKETS.

BEHIND JONES, IN THE CUPOLA OF THE LUTHERAN THEOLOGICAL SEMINARY AT GETTYSBURG, STOOD UNION CAVALRY GEN. JOHN BUFORD. BUFORD AND HIS TROOPERS HAD REACHED THE TOWN THE DAY BEFORE AND, RECOGNIZING THE VALUE OF THE POSITION, WERE DETERMINED TO HOLD IT UNTIL SUPPORT ARRIVED.

THE ARMY OF THE POTOMAC WAS STRUNG OUT FOR MILES TO THE SOUTH, COMING UP TO FIND BOBBY LEE. DESPITE LEE'S ORDER NOT TO ENGAGE THE ENEMY UNTIL THE ARMY OF NORTHERN VIRGINIA HAD GATHERED, HETH'S WAS COMING IN AND, AS BUFORD HAD PREDICTED TO A SUBORDINATE THE DAY BEFORE, HE WAS COMING IN "BOOMING," THINKING HE COULD QUICKLY BRUSH THIS THIN LINE OF CAVALRY ASIDE.

HETH'S FORCES FACED 3 RIDGES THAT CROSSED PERPENDICULAR ACROSS THEIR PATH: HERR RIDGE, MCPHERSON'S RIDGE, AND SEMINARY RIDGE, WITH THE LUTHERAN SEMINARY ON ITS CROWN. HE CROSSED HERR RIDGE AT ABOUT 8:00 AM WITH THE BRIGADES OF JOSEPH DAVIS AND JAMES ARCHER IN THE LEAD. HIS INTENTIONS WERE TO PUSH THE CAVALRY ASIDE AND OCCUPY THE TOWN.

BUFORD'S 2,749 TROOPS WERE FACING 7,461 REBELS, BUT THEY WERE ARMED WITH BREECH-LOADING SHARPS CARBINES AND COULD FIRE 8 TO 10 ROUNDS A MINUTE. BUFORD INTENDED TO HOLD ON UNTIL GEN. JOHN F. REYNOLDS ARRIVED WITH THE FEDERAL LEFT WING AND THE I CORPS.

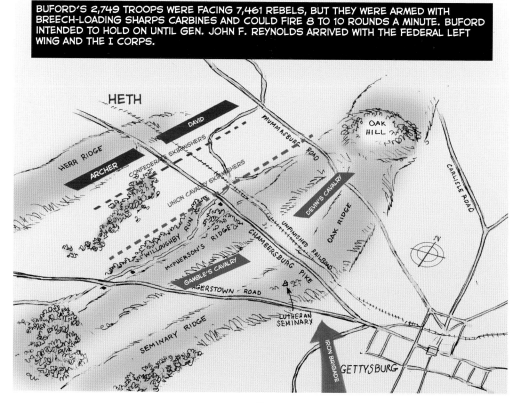

BY 9:00 AM, BUFORD COULD SEE THAT HIS CAVALRYMEN WERE BEING FORCED TO RETREAT ACROSS WILLOUGHBY RUN. THEN HE LOOKED DOWN ...

REYNOLDS! THE DEVIL TO PAY!

WITH BUFORD'S PROMISE TO HOLD ON A LITTLE LONGER, REYNOLDS SENT WORD FOR JAMES WADSWORTH TO MOVE HIS DIVISION UP TO THE LINE AS QUICKLY AS POSSIBLE.

HE ALSO SENT A MESSAGE BACK TO MEADE THAT HE INTENDED TO HOLD THE REBELS "INCH BY INCH." THE MESSAGE REACHED MEADE AT TANEYTOWN, 15 MILES TO THE SOUTH.

GOOD! THAT IS JUST LIKE REYNOLDS. HE WILL HOLD ON TO THE BITTER END.

MEADE HELD REYNOLDS IN HIGH REGARD, AS DID THE REST OF THE ARMY.

REYNOLDS RODE BACK AND MET HIS ADVANCING CORPS ABOUT A MILE SOUTH OF TOWN. HE URGED THEM FORWARD.

SOLOMON MEREDITH'S 1ST BRIGADE OF THE 1ST CORPS, KNOWN AS THE IRON BRIGADE, LOADED THIER WEAPONS AS THEY DOUBLE-TIMED FORWARD.

THEY REACHED THE CREST OF MCPHERSON'S RIDGE AT ABOUT 10:00 AM.

AS THE IRON BRIGADE MOVED TO THE FRONT, THEY WERE CHEERED BY THE EXHAUSTED CAVALRYMEN.

WE HAVE GOT THEM NOW!

GO IN AND GIVE THEM HELL!

REYNOLDS DIRECTED THE 2ND MAINE ARTILLERY INTO POSITION AND MORE OF WADSWORTH'S BRIGADES INTO THE LINE.

SUDDENLY, REYNOLDS FELL FROM HIS HORSE FACEDOWN ON THE GROUND. A MINI BALL HAD STRUCK HIM BEHIND THE RIGHT EAR ...

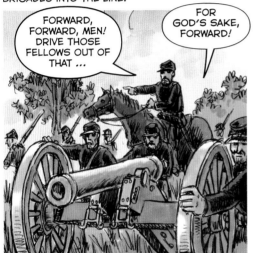

FORWARD, FORWARD, MEN! DRIVE THOSE FELLOWS OUT OF THAT ...

FOR GOD'S SAKE, FORWARD!

... HE WAS DEAD AT 42.

HETH SENT IN THE BRIGADES OF JOSEPH DAVIS AND JAMES ARCHER, MEN FROM MISSISSIPPI AND NORTH CAROLINA. THEY THOUGHT THEY WERE GOING UP AGAINST A THIN LINE OF CAVALRY.

THERE ARE THOSE DAMNED BLACK-HATTED FELLOWS AGAIN ...

... TAIN'T NO MILITIA! IT'S THE ARMY OF THE POTOMAC.

THE IRON BRIGADE'S 19TH INDIANA AND 24TH MICHIGAN HIT ARCHER'S BRIGADE HARD, TURNING HIS RIGHT FLANK. THE CONFEDERATES QUICKLY PULLED BACK ACROSS WILLOUGHBY RUN.

THE IRON BRIGADE TOOK MANY PRISONERS, INCLUDING ARCHER HIMSELF, ROUGHLY COLLARED BY PVT. PATRICK MALONEY OF THE 2ND WISCONSIN.

ON THE WAY TO THE REAR, ARCHER WAS SPOTTED BY HIS OLD ARMY FRIEND, ABNER DOUBLEDAY.

GOOD MORNING, ARCHER! I'M GLAD TO SEE YOU.

WELL, I AM NOT GLAD TO SEE YOU BY A DAMNED SIGHT!

NORTH OF THE CHAMBERSBURG PIKE AND AN UNFINISHED RAILROAD LINE, 2 OF THE REGIMENTS OF LYSANDER CUTLER WERE BEING FLANKED AND PUSHED BACK BY DAVIS'S CONFEDERATES.

TWO RED-PANTED NEW YORK REGIMENTS AND THE 6TH WISCONSIN OF THE IRON BRIGADE PUSHED NORTH ACROSS THE PIKE, BREAKING UP THE REBEL ADVANCE.

THE CONFEDERATES FELL BACK INTO A RAILROAD CUT THAT GAVE THEM GOOD PROTECTION FIRING OVER THE RIM. BUT THE WISCONSIN MEN WERE DETERMINED TO DRIVE THEM FROM IT.

ALTHOUGH TAKING HEAVY CASUALTIES, THE 6TH WISCONSIN SURROUNDED THE CUT, CAUSING 250 REBELS TO SURRENDER AND CAPTURING THE COLORS OF THE 2ND MISSISSIPPI.

AS 11:00 AM NEARED, A STRANGE QUIET SETTLED OVER THE BATTLEFIELD, BROKEN ONLY BY AN OCCASIONAL SHOT FROM SKIRMISHERS OR THE MOANS OF THE WOUNDED. DAVIS AND ARCHER PULLED THEIR BLEEDING BRIGADES BACK TO HERR RIDGE. THEY BOTH HAD LOST HALF THEIR MEN, EITHER CAPTURED OR SHOT ...

... AND IT WAS STILL BEFORE NOON.

THE FIRST DAY GATHERING STORM

AMBROSE POWELL HILL, WHO LEE ONCE CALLED HIS "FIGHTENEST" DIVISION COMMANDER, WAS IN CASHTOWN, SICK FROM SOME UNKNOWN AILMENT, WHEN THE FIGHTING IN GETTYSBURG BEGAN. THIS UNRECOGNIZED SICKNESS WOULD AFFECT HIM FOR THE REST OF THE WAR. BUT ON JULY 1, IT DID NOT KEEP HIM FROM RUSHING WILLIAM PENDER DORSEY'S DIVISION EAST TO AID HETH AT GETTYSBURG.

SOON, THE CONFEDERATE CORPS OF RICHARD EWELL WOULD BEGAN TO ARRIVE FROM THE NORTH.

MEANWHILE, THE FEDERAL FORCES WERE ADJUSTING THEIR FORCES AROUND GETTYSBURG, A SITUATION FURTHER COMPLICATED BY THE SPOTTING OF CONFEDERATE FORCES MOVING IN FROM THE NORTH.

OLIVER O. HOWARD HAD REACHED THE BATTLEFIELD AND, FINDING THAT REYNOLDS WAS DEAD, TOOK OVERALL COMMAND OF THE UNION FORCES. HE SENT WORD FOR HIS XI CORPS TO BE BROUGHT UP IMMEDIATELY.

AT ABOUT 12:30 PM, 16 CONFEDERATE CANNONS OPENED FIRE FROM A HIGH POINT CALLED OAK HILL.

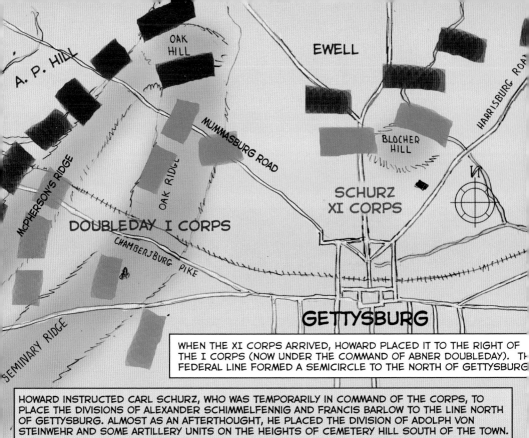

A. P. HILL

OAK HILL

EWELL

HARRISBURG ROAD

MUNNASBURG ROAD

BLOCHER HILL

McPHERSON'S RIDGE

OAK RIDGE

SCHURZ XI CORPS

DOUBLEDAY I CORPS

CHAMBERSBURG PIKE

SEMINARY RIDGE

GETTYSBURG

WHEN THE XI CORPS ARRIVED, HOWARD PLACED IT TO THE RIGHT OF THE I CORPS (NOW UNDER THE COMMAND OF ABNER DOUBLEDAY). TH FEDERAL LINE FORMED A SEMICIRCLE TO THE NORTH OF GETTYSBURG

HOWARD INSTRUCTED CARL SCHURZ, WHO WAS TEMPORARILY IN COMMAND OF THE CORPS, TO PLACE THE DIVISIONS OF ALEXANDER SCHIMMELFENNIG AND FRANCIS BARLOW TO THE LINE NORTH OF GETTYSBURG. ALMOST AS AN AFTERTHOUGHT, HE PLACED THE DIVISION OF ADOLPH VON STEINWEHR AND SOME ARTILLERY UNITS ON THE HEIGHTS OF CEMETERY HILL SOUTH OF THE TOWN.

BOYS, I WANT YOU TO HOLD THIS POSITION AT ALL HAZARDS.

MEANWHILE, COURIERS WERE TAKING MESSAGES BACK AND FORTH AMONG THE CONFEDERATE COMMANDERS. EWELL, RESPONDING TO HILL'S SITUATION, SENT THE DIVISIONS OF RODES AND EARLY SOUTH TO GETTYSBURG RATHER THAN THE SCHEDULED RENDEZVOUS AT CASHTOWN. LEE APPROVED THIS CHANGE ...

... BUT WARNED AGAINST COMMITTING TO A GENERAL ENGAGEMENT.

SCHURZ, NOT KNOWING FROM WHAT DIRECTION THE ENEMY WOULD ATTACK, PLACED THE 2 DIVISIONS ASSIGNED TO HIM IN A THIN, MILE-LONG LINE THAT DID NOT FULLY CONNECT WITH THE RIGHT FLANK OF THE I CORPS. A QUARTER-MILE GAP LAY BETWEEN THE 2 CORPS.

SUDDENLY, SHORTLY BEFORE 2:00 PM, THE 7,983-MAN DIVISION OF MAJ. GEN. ROBERT RODES EMERGED FROM THE WOODS TO THE NORTHEAST.

RODES HAD SPOTTED THE GAP BETWEEN THE 2 UNION CORPS. DESPITE LEE'S ORDER TO AVOID A GENERAL ENGAGEMENT, RODES DECIDED TO ATTACK WITH ALL HIS FORCES AT HAND. THE OPPORTUNITY TO SPLIT THE UNION WAS TOO GREAT.

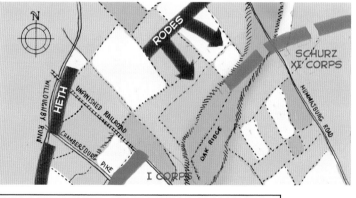

RODE'S ATTACK WENT IN POORLY COORDINATED, UNDER BRIGADE COMMANDERS BOTH RELIABLE AND LESS THAN DEPENDABLE. BUT THE MOST IMPORTANT ELEMENT WAS ON THE UNION SIDE IN THE FORM OF HENRY BAXTER'S BRIGADE. THESE MEN OF NEW YORK, PENNSYLVANIA, AND MAINE WERE ONLY 1,400 STRONG, BUT THEY WERE BEHIND A STOUT STONE WALL ALONG THE MUMMASBURG ROAD.

IN A MATTER OF MINUTES, RODES LOST NEARLY 700 MEN FROM THE BRIGADE OF EDWARD O'NEAL. HE WAS INFURIATED TO FIND THAT SEVERAL OF HIS REGIMENTAL COMMANDERS HAD STAYED WITH RESERVE UNITS AND NOT EVEN GONE IN WITH THEIR MEN.

LYSANDER CUTLER'S BRIGADE, OF THE I CORPS, WHICH HAD BEEN ANCHORED ON THE RIGHT OF THE IRON BRIGADE, SHIFTED TO THE RIGHT AND HOOKED UP WITH BAXTER'S BRIGADE BEHIND THEIR STONE WALL. CUTLER'S MEN HAD THE ADVANTAGE OF YET ANOTHER STONE WALL.

AS O'NEAL'S SURVIVORS FELL BACK, ALFRED IVERSON'S BRIGADE OF NORTH CAROLINIANS ADVANCED IN THEIR 4 REGIMENTS ABREAST. THE MEN LED BY BAXTER AND CUTLER WAITED UNTIL THE CONFEDERATES WERE WITHIN 80 YARDS BEFORE THEY ROSE UP AND OPENED FIRE.

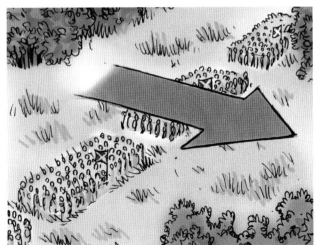

MORE THAN 500 OF IVERSON'S MEN WENT DOWN AT ONCE IN A "LINE AS STRAIGHT AS DRESS PARADE." BAXTER'S BRIGADE SUDDENLY CAME UP OVER THE WALL IN A FIERY COUNTERATTACK.

IVERSON'S MEN BECAME UNGLUED, EITHER FALLING BACK OR SURRENDERING. THE FEDERAL MEN CAPTURED MORE THAN 400 PRISONERS.

IVERSON HIMSELF BECAME DISTRAUGHT AND HAD TO BE LED FROM THE BATTLEFIELD. HE HAD SENT IN 1,384 MEN. 15 MINUTES LATER, HE HAD FEWER THAN 400.

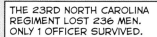

THE 23RD NORTH CAROLINA REGIMENT LOST 236 MEN. ONLY 1 OFFICER SURVIVED.

THE NORTH CAROLINA BRIGADES OF JUNIUS DANIEL AND STEPHEN DODSON RAMSEUR MOVED INTO THE BATTLE. DANIEL MOVED TO HIS RIGHT, INTENDING TO FLANK CUTLER AND BAXTER.

IT MIGHT HAVE WORKED, TOO, EXCEPT FOR THE UNFINISHED RAILROAD CUT AND THE BRIGADE OF ROY STONE JUST BEYOND IT. THESE WERE THE 143RD, 149TH, AND THE 150TH PENNSYLVANIA REGIMENTS THAT MADE UP THE BUCKTAIL BRIGADE. THEY WERE PENNSYLVANIA DEER HUNTERS WHO WORE DEER TAILS ON THEIR HATS.

THEIR FIRE STAGGERED DANIEL'S ATTACK.

72-YEAR-OLD COBBLER JOHN BURNS, A GETTYSBURG NATIVE, HEARD THE NOISE OF BATTLE AND DECIDED IT COULDN'T GO ON WITHOUT HIM TAKING PART IN IT. HE TOOK HIS OLD FLINTLOCK AND HEADED TOWARD THE SOUND OF BATTLE.

HE JOINED UP WITH THE 150TH PENNSYLVANIA AND LATER WITH THE IRON BRIGADE.

THE BUCKTAILS ATTACKED DANIEL'S BRIGADES BUT WERE BEATEN BACK BY ARTILLERY FROM A. P. HILL'S CORPS TO THE WEST.

THE SAVAGE FIGHT WENT BACK AND FORTH. BY THE END OF THE DAY, 2/3 OF THE BUCKTAILS WERE DOWN, AND MANY OF THEIR OFFICERS HAD BEEN KILLED.

RAMSEUR WAS ALSO HAVING A DIFFICULT TIME WITH HIS ATTACK AGAINST THE DIVISION OF JOHN C. ROBINSON, A CAREER SOLDIER WHO SOME CALLED THE "HAIRIEST MAN IN THE ARMY." CASUALTIES ON BOTH SIDES WERE HEAVY, AND THE UNION UNITS LOST MANY OF THEIR OFFICERS.

AMMUNITION WAS RUNNING SO LOW THAT ROBINSON HIMSELF WAS COLLECTING CARTRIDGE BOXES FROM THE DEAD.

AS THE REBELS MOVED IN FROM ALL SIDES, THE MEN TORE THEIR FLAGS TO SHREDS.

BY NOW GENERAL LEE HAD REACHED THE FIELD, ANNOYED THAT HIS INSTRUCTIONS HAD NOT BEEN FOLLOWED.

I AM NOT PREPARED TO BRING ON A GENERAL ENGAGEMENT TODAY ...

... GENERAL LONGSTREET'S FORCES ARE NOT UP.

LEE THEN SAW DUST FROM BEYOND THE RIGHT FLANK OF THE FEDERAL XI CORPS. IT WAS THE ARRIVAL JUBAL EARLY'S DIVISION. THE UNION LINE WAS BENDING BACK ON ITSELF. LEE THOUGHT THAT IF EARLY COULD ASSAULT THE FEDERAL RIGHT, AND IF A. P. HILL COULD RENEW HIS ASSAULT...

...ALTHOUGH ALL HIS FORCES WERE NOT AVAILABLE, LEE DECIDED TO RESPOND TO THIS OPPORTUNITY. HE QUICKLY ORDERED HETH, SUPPORTED BY PENDER, TO ATTACK.

THE HETH-PENDER ATTACK BEGAN AT ABOUT 2:45 PM. THEY MOVED DOWN TOWARD WILLOUGHBY RUN 12 REGIMENTS ABREAST.

NEAR THE CENTER OF THE LINE WAS THE 26TH NORTH CAROLINA. THE REGIMENT HAD NOT BEEN WITH THE ARMY LONG AND STILL NUMBERED OVER 800 MEN, LOOKING MORE LIKE A BRIGADE THAN A REGIMENT.

THEIR COMMANDER, COL. HENRY K. BURGWYN, WAS ONLY 22 YEARS OLD.

THEY MOVED THROUGH LIGHT WOODS, SPLASHED ACROSS THE RUN, AND STARTED UP MCPHERSON'S RIDGE. THEY CAME UP AGAINST THE IRON BRIGADE'S 24TH MICHIGAN.

BOTH SIDES OPENED UP WITH A BLISTERING FIRE.

ON THE UNION LEFT, A FEDERAL BATTERY BEGAN TO FIRE CANISTER INTO THE CONFEDERATE LINE.

THE DAMAGE WAS DEVASTATING.

THE FIRE FROM BOTH THE ARTILLERY AND THE IRON BRIGADE TORE INTO THE 26TH, KILLING THEIR COLOR BEARERS. TIME AND TIME AGAIN, MEN PICKED UP THE FLAGS ONLY TO BE CUT DOWN LIKE THE MEN BEFORE THEM. DURING THE ADVANCE, AT LEAST A DOZEN COLOR BEARERS WENT DOWN, INCLUDING COLONEL BURGWYN.

AFTER THE ADVANCE, ONLY 216 MEN OF THE ORIGINAL 800 OF THE 26TH WERE FIT FOR DUTY.

THE 24TH MICHIGAN SUFFERED SIMILAR LOSSES ...

... AND THE IRON BRIGADE BEGAN TO FALL BACK TOWARD GETTYSBURG.

NORTH OF THE TOWN, WHERE THE CARLISLE ROAD FORKS, THE GEORGIA BRIGADE OF GEORGE P. DOLES WAITED OUT THE SKIRMISHERS. HE KNEW THAT JUBAL EARLY'S DIVISION WOULD BE COMING IN AT ANY MOMENT, AND HE WAS WAITING FOR THEM TO HOOK UP TO HIS LEFT BEFORE ADVANCING.

THE GROUND AHEAD OF HIM WAS MOSTLY FLAT FARMLAND EXCEPT FOR A FEATURELESS HILL CALLED BLOCHER'S KNOLL. HIS SKIRMISHERS SAT ACROSS IT.

FACING HIM WAS THE UNION BRIGADE OF WLODZIMIERZ KRZYZANOWSKI, A POLISH NOBLEMAN WHO'D HAD TO FLEE POLAND WHEN A REVOLT HE WAS PART OF FAILED.

TO HIS RIGHT WAS THE DIVISION OF NEW YORK LAWYER FRANCIS BARLOW, WHO'D DECIDED THAT BLOCHER'S KNOLL WOULD BE A GOOD PLACE TO ANCHOR HIS RIGHT FLANK.

AT ABOUT 3:00 PM, BARLOW ADVANCED THE BRIGADES OF ADELBERT AMES AND LEOPOLD VON GILSA TO TAKE IT.

IN DOING THIS, BARLOW OPENED HIS LEFT TO DOLE'S BRIGADE. TO CORRECT THE LINE, CARL SCHURZ, COMMANDING XI CORPS, ORDERED KRZYZANOWSKI FORWARD. THIS MOVEMENT CAUSED A VIOLENT REACTION FROM DOLES, WHO LASHED OUT WITH HIS 1,324-MAN BRIGADE AGAINST THE MORE THAN 5,000 YANKEES WHO FACED HIM.

THIS MAY HAVE SEEMED FOOLHARDY, BUT AT THAT MOMENT JUBAL EARLY ARRIVED IN THE FORM OF THE BRIGADES OF JOHN B. GORDON AND HARRY T. HAYS.

ATLANTA LAWYER GORDON LED HIS MEN WHILE RIDING A COAL-BLACK STALLION; THE MEN SAID IT LOOKED LIKE WAR ITSELF.

THE GEORGIANS SLAMMED INTO BARLOW'S MEN. THE UNION LINE BENT ...

34

... AND THEN BROKE, FALLING BACK TOWARD GETTYSBURG.

AFTER THE ADVANCE MOVED ON SOUTH, GORDON FOUND A UNION OFFICER WITH A TERRIBLE CHEST WOUND.

BOTH MEN FELT BARLOW WOULD DIE. GORDON PROMISED HE WOULD CONTACT BARLOW'S WIFE. HE THEN PLACED THE UNION OFFICER IN THE SHADE OF A NEARBY TREE.

IT WAS FRANCIS BARLOW.

LEGEND HAS IT THAT THESE MEN WOULD MEET AGAIN.

BY NOW, ALL CONFEDERATE UNITS WERE COMBINED IN A GENERAL ADVANCE. LEE, NOW ON THE FIELD, SAW THE IMPORTANCE OF CAPTURING THE HEIGHTS BELOW GETTYSBURG. A. P. HILL WAS ORDERED TO RENEW HIS ATTACK, BUT HE FELT HIS MEN WERE WORN OUT AND ALMOST OUT OF AMMUNITION.

LEE SENT HIS AIDE, MAJ. WALTER TAYLOR, TO FIND GENERAL EWELL. HIS ORDERS WERE TO "PRESS THOSE PEOPLE IN ORDER TO SECURE THE POSSESSION OF THE HEIGHTS ... IF PRACTICABLE."

AT 1:00 PM IN TANEYTOWN, MEADE FIRST GOT WORD OF THE FIGHTING IN GETTYSBURG. HE SENT II CORPS COMMANDER WINFIELD SCOTT HANCOCK TO TAKE COMMAND UNTIL MEADE GOT THERE AND TO STUDY THE GROUND.

HANCOCK ARRIVED IN GETTYSBURG AT ABOUT 4:30 AND WITNESSED THE UNION TROOPS FALLING BACK THROUGH THE TOWN. HE FOUND GENERALS HOWARD AND DOUBLEDAY AT THE ENTRANCE GATE OF EVERGREEN CEMETERY.

A SHORT ARGUMENT ENSUED BETWEEN HOWARD AND HANCOCK DEALING WITH WHO WAS IN CHARGE.

GENERAL MEADE HAS ORDERED ME TO TAKE COMMAND.

YOU CANNOT GIVE ORDERS HERE. I AM IN COMMAND AND I RANK YOU!

THEY BOTH FINALLY AGREED THAT THE GROUND WAS VERY WELL SUITED FOR DEFENSE.

ONE OF THE MEMBERS OF THE 154TH NEW YORK REGIMENT WAS SGT. AMOS HUMISTON, A HARNESS MAKER FROM WESTERN NEW YORK, MARRIED AND FATHER OF 3 CHILDREN.

WHEN THE PICTURE OF THESE 3 CHILDREN, 2 BOYS AND A GIRL, WERE PUBLISHED IN A PHILADELPHIA NEWSPAPER, IT BEGAN A NATIONWIDE SEARCH.

SOMETIME DURING THE BATTLE, HUMISTON WAS MORTALLY WOUNDED.

WHEN HUMISTON'S BODY WAS DISCOVERED 3 DAYS LATER, THEY FOUND NO IDENTIFICATION EXCEPT FOR AN AMBROTYPE OF 3 CHILDREN CLUTCHED IN HIS HAND.

CHILDREN OF THE BATTLE

THE FEDERAL TROOPS FELL BACK, ABANDONING GETTYSBURG. EWELL HAD NOT YET ORDERED AN ATTACK TO TAKE THE HIGH GROUND TO THE SOUTH, THE HIGH GROUND THAT HOWARD HAD ORDERED VON STEINWEHR TO DEFEND.

EWELL AND GORDON WERE RIDING THROUGH GETTYSBURG WHEN A STRAY BULLET HIT EWELL IN THE LEG, CAUSING HIS HORSE TO REEL.

ARE YOU HURT, SIR?

WHAP!

NO, NO ...

IT DON'T HURT A BIT TO GET SHOT IN A WOODEN LEG.

JAMES LONGSTREET FINALLY ARRIVED AT LEE'S HEADQUARTERS AT ABOUT 5:00 PM, WELL AHEAD OF HIS CORPS. HE STUDIED THE BATTLEFIELD AND TOLD HIS COMMANDER THAT HE FELT THEY HAD A PERFECT OPPORTUNITY TO SLIP AROUND THE UNION LEFT AND FIND GROUND BETWEEN THE ARMY OF THE POTOMAC AND WASHINGTON. THAT WAY THEY WOULD BE FIGHTING A DEFENSIVE BATTLE.

BUT LEE HAD A COMPLETELY DIFFERENT ATTITUDE ABOUT THE SITUATION.

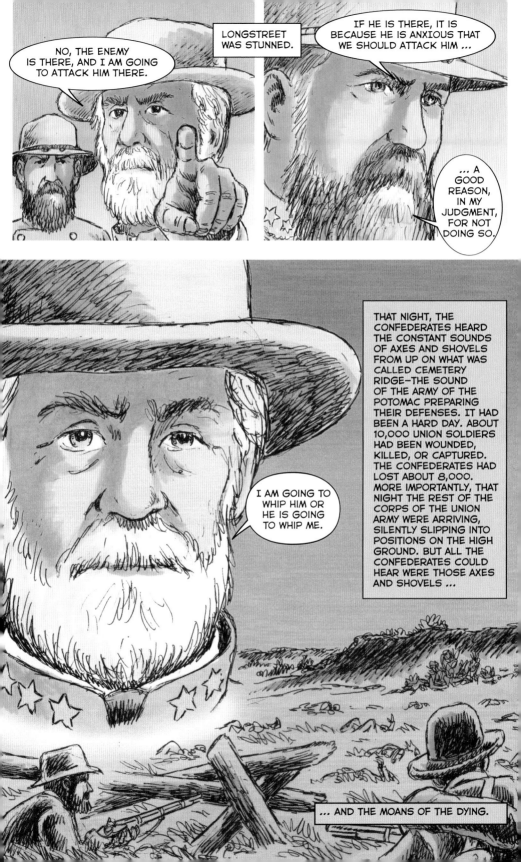

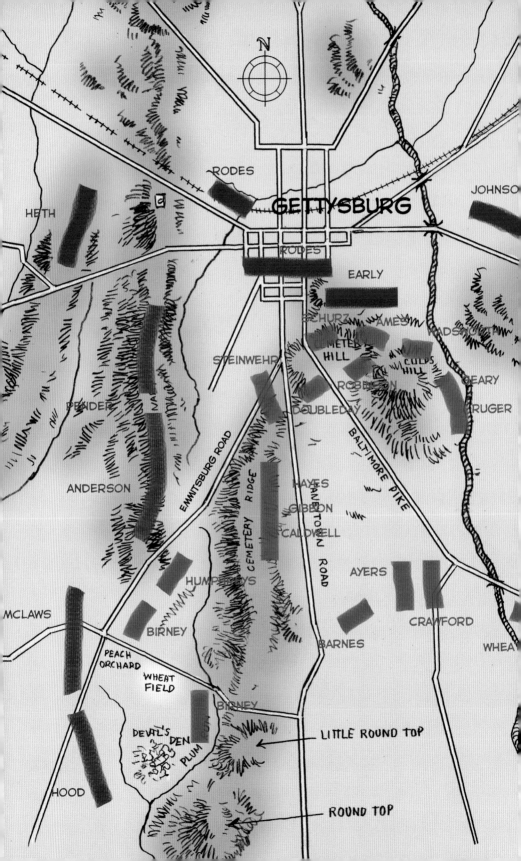

BY THE EARLY MORNING HOURS OF JULY 2, JEB STUART AND HIS 4,800 CAVALRYMEN HAD SPENT 7 DAYS ON A FORAY THAT ACCOMPLISHED LITTLE MORE THAN WEARING OUT HIS MEN AND HORSES. EVERY TIME THE SITUATION CALLED FOR STUART TO TURN WEST AND STAY CLOSE TO LEE'S ARMY, HE WOULD TAKE THE MORE DANGEROUS COURSE AND RIDE FARTHER AND FARTHER SOUTH AND EAST, FINALLY TURNING NORTH.

FINALLY, EXHAUSTED AND SLOWED DOWN BY A CAPTURED 125-WAGON MULE TRAIN, THEY NEARED THE ARMY OF NORTHERN VIRGINIA, WHOM HE HAD PROMISED TO KEEP INFORMED OF THE FEDERAL'S MOVEMENTS ... AND FAILED.

AT 5:00 AM THAT MORNING, GENERAL LONGSTREET JOINED GENERAL LEE ON SEMINARY RIDGE, WHERE THE COMMANDER WAS STUDYING THE FEDERAL DEFENSES ON CEMETERY RIDGE.

LONGSTREET WANTED AGAIN TO PRESS HIS CASE ABOUT MOVING THE ARMY SOUTH, THEN EAST, TO ATTACK ENEMY'S REAR.

LEE AGAIN COURTEOUSLY BUT FIRMLY REJECTED LONGSTREET'S PLAN.

HE WOULD NOT CHANGE HIS MIND: HIS BLOOD WAS UP!

LEE GATHERED HIS COMMANDERS TOGETHER WHOSE UNITS WERE ON THE FIELD. SEVERAL MAJOR UNITS HAD NOW YET ARRIVED, LIKE PICKETT'S DIVISION OF LONGSTREET'S CORPS. LEE HAD NOT WANTED TO COMMIT TO BATTLE UNTIL HIS WHOLE ARMY WAS GATHERED, BUT BECAUSE STUART HAD NOT KEPT HIM AWARE OF THE FEDERAL'S MOVEMENTS, THEY WERE IN THE PRESENT SITUATION AND HAD NO CHOICE.

LEE LAID OUT HIS PLAN. HE WANTED TO ATTACK WITH 2 DIVISIONS NORTHEAST UP THE EMMITSBURG ROAD ON CEMETERY RIDGE: JOHN BELL HOOD'S ON THE RIGHT, LAFAYETTE MCLAWS'S ON THE LEFT. HE WANTED THE ASSAULT MADE IN "ECHELONS," FROM RIGHT TO LEFT, EACH BRIGADE STRIKING ONE AFTER THE OTHER.

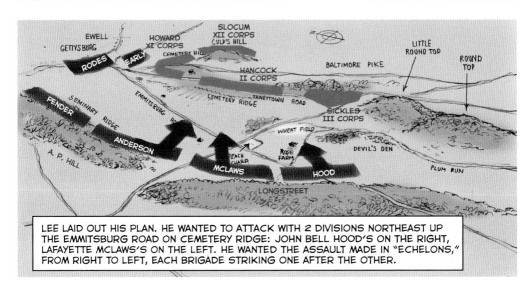

AT THAT POINT IN TIME, THERE WERE 2 HILLS ON THE SOUTHERN EDGE OF CEMETERY RIDGE THAT THE UNION FORCES HAD NOT OCCUPIED. THESE WERE CALLED ROUND TOP AND LITTLE ROUND TOP. AS LONG AS THESE HILLS WERE NOT OCCUPIED BY THE FEDERALS, LEE HAD NO CONCERN FOR THEM.

THE MEETING WAS OVER AT 10:00 AM, AND LEE TOLD LONGSTREET THAT HE SHOULD START MOVING HIS FORCES.

SEVERAL OF HIS COMRADES NOTICED THAT LEE SEEMED OUT OF SORTS THAT MORNING, WALKING AS THOUGH HE WERE "WEAK AND IN PAIN."

IT WAS NOON BEFORE LONGSTREET BEGAN TO MOVE HIS CORPS, AND HE HAD DIFFICULTY FINDING A ROUTE TO HIS JUMP-OFF POINT, WHICH WAS NOT IN CLEAR OBSERVATION. SEVERAL ROUTES TURNED OUT TO BE IN PLAIN VIEW, AND THE UNITS HAD TO RETRACE THEIR TRACKS SEVERAL MILES AND BEGIN AGAIN MOVING SOUTH.

FINALLY, AT AROUND 3:30 PM, HOOD AND MCLAWS REACHED THEIR ASSIGNED JUMP-OFF POINT.

NOT LONG AFTER LONGSTREET LEFT WITH HIS CORPS, STUART ARRIVED AHEAD OF HIS CAVALRY.

I HAVE NOT HEARD A WORD FROM YOU FOR DAYS, AND YOU ARE THE EYES AND EARS OF MY ARMY.

I HAVE BROUGHT YOU 125 WAGONS AND THEIR TEAMS, GENERAL.

LEE GREETED STUART WITH AN ICY STARE, AND THE CAVALRYMAN KNEW HE WAS IN TROUBLE.

WHEN HE SAW HOW HIS MANNER HURT STUART, LEE SOFTENED.

YES, AND THEY ARE AN IMPEDIMENT TO ME NOW.

LET ME ASK YOUR HELP NOW. WE WILL NOT DISCUSS THIS MATTER FURTHER ...

... HELP ME FIGHT THESE PEOPLE.

GENERAL MEADE HAD ARRIVED IN GETTYSBURG A FEW HOURS AFTER MIDNIGHT, AND HE HAD BEEN UP ALL NIGHT PLACING HIS TROOPS ALONG THE RIDGE. ALL OF HIS CORPS HAD ARRIVED EXCEPT FOR JOHN SEDGWICK'S VI CORPS, THE LARGEST IN THE ARMY AT 14,000.

SEDGWICK HAD SENT WORD THAT HIS CORPS WOULD BE IN GETTYSBURG BY 4:00 PM ON JULY 2 IF THEY HAD TO MARCH ALL NIGHT.

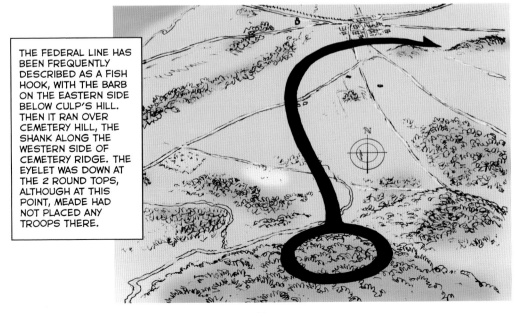

THE FEDERAL LINE HAS BEEN FREQUENTLY DESCRIBED AS A FISH HOOK, WITH THE BARB ON THE EASTERN SIDE BELOW CULP'S HILL. THEN IT RAN OVER CEMETERY HILL, THE SHANK ALONG THE WESTERN SIDE OF CEMETERY RIDGE. THE EYELET WAS DOWN AT THE 2 ROUND TOPS, ALTHOUGH AT THIS POINT, MEADE HAD NOT PLACED ANY TROOPS THERE.

THE III CORPS COMMANDER, MAJ. GEN. DANIEL E. SICKLES, WAS A TAMMANY HALL POLITICIAN WHO HAD LIMITED MILITARY EXPERIENCE, AND HE OWED HIS RANK TO HIS POLITICAL CONNECTIONS. HIS CORPS HAD BEEN ASSIGNED THE AREA TO THE LEFT OF THE HANCOCK'S II CORPS.

HE DID NOT LIKE THE POSITION: HERE CEMETERY RIGE SLOPPED DOWN TO WHAT COULD BE CALLED THE VALLEY FLOOR.

TO THE SOUTH WERE THE ROUND TOPS THAT LOOKED TOO STEEP AND ROCKY TO PLACE ARTILLERY. BUT TO THE WEST WAS SOME HIGH GROUND, A SHORT, FLAT-TOPPED RIDGE WITH A PEACH ORCHARD THAT LOOKED LIKE A GOOD PLACE TO PLACE HIS ARTILLERY.

AT ABOUT 3:00 PM, SICKLES MOVED HIS VETERAN DIVISION FORWARD.

THE OFFICERS OF II CORPS WATCHED FROM THEIR POSITION TO THE NORTH AND ADMIRED HOW WELL THEY MARCHED FORWARD.

HANCOCK WAS LESS IMPRESSED.

WAIT A MOMENT, AND YOU'LL SEE THEM TUMBLING BACK.

AT 3:30 PM, A CONFEDERATE CANNON SIGNALED THE OPENING OF LONGSTREET'S ATTACK. ON HEARING THIS, MEADE REALIZED THAT HE HAD NEGLECTED THE LEFT WING. HE ORDERED SYKES'S V CORPS FORWARD TO SUPPORT SICKLES.

MEADE RODE TO THE FRONT AND WAS SHOCKED TO SEE WHERE SICKLES HAD PLACED HIS CORPS. HE SENT THE ARMY'S CHIEF TOPOGRAPHICAL ENGINEER, BRIG. GEN. GOUVERNEUR WARREN SOUTH, TO ACCESS THE ROUND TOPS.

WARREN REACHED THE LITTLE ROUND TOP AND FOUND THAT A UNION SIGNAL STATION WAS ALL THAT OCCUPIED IT. HAVING A GOOD SENSE OF GROUND, THE ENGINEER SENT WORD TO GENERAL SYKES TO SEND A BRIGADE IMMEDIATELY TO OCCUPY THE HILL.

WHEN JOHN BELL HOOD BEGAN HIS ATTACK, HE REALIZED THAT ATTACKING UP THE EMMITSBURG ROAD WOULD BE SUICIDAL, SO HE DIRECTED HIS ATTACK DUE EAST TOWARD THE ROUND TOPS IN HOPES OF FLANKING THE FEDERAL LINE.

ON HOOD'S FAR RIGHT WAS EVANDER LAW'S ALABAMA BRIGADE, SUPPORTED BY TEXAS AND GEORGIA UNITS. THEY WERE GETTING HEAVY FIRE FROM THE 2ND U.S. SHARPSHOOTERS, WHO WERE FIRING FROM BIG ROUND TOP'S HEAVILY WOODED SLOPES.

TO CLEAR THEM OUT, THE 15TH AND 47TH ALABAMA CHARGED THE STEEP, WOODED, ROCKY SLOPE.

WHEN THEY REACHED THE TOP, COL. WILLIAM C. OATES REALIZED THAT THEY WERE ON THE HIGHEST POINT FOR MILES.

DOWN BELOW, GENERAL HOOD'S LEFT ARM WAS SHATTERED BY A SHELL BURST. COMMAND OF HIS DIVISION SHIFTED TO EVANDER LAW.

LAW'S ORDERS TO COLONEL OATES WERE TO ABANDON HIS POSITION ON THE BIG ROUND TOP, DESCEND TO THE NORTH, AND TAKE THE LITTLE ROUND TOP.

OATES AND HIS MEN DESCENDED DOWN THE BIG ROUND TOP ONTO THE 500-YARD SADDLE THAT LED TO THE LITTLE ROUND TOP. HOOKING UP WITH HIM ON HIS LEFT WERE THE 47TH ALABAMA, 4TH ALABAMA, 5TH TEXAS, AND 4TH TEXAS. SO FAR, OATES HAD NOT SEEN A SINGLE ENEMY SOLDIER.

MEANWHILE, ABOUT A QUARTER MILE TO THE WEST, HENRY BENNING'S GEORGIA BRIGADE AND JEROME B. ROBERTSON'S TEXAS BRIGADE ADVANCED INTO A ROCKY MAZE OF BOULDERS CALLED THE DEVIL'S DEN, NAMED AFTER A LEGENDARY OLD SNAKE THAT LOCALS SAID LIVED THERE.

THE DEVIL'S DEN WAS DEFENDED BY A COMBINATION OF NEW YORK, PENNSYLVANIA, MAINE, AND NEW JERSEY MEN AND THE BATTERY OF THE 4TH NEW YORK.

AT THIS CLOSE RANGE, THE BATTERY DID TERRIBLE WORK. IT WAS A SHELL FROM THIS BATTERY THAT HAD WOUNDED GENERAL HOOD.

TO THE RIGHT OF THE BATTERY WAS THE 124TH NEW YORK. THE MEN WERE FROM ORANGE COUNTY, SO THEY WORE AN ORANGE RIBBON ON THEIR COATS AND CALLED THEMSELVES "ORANGE BLOSSOMS."

THEIR COLONEL WAS AUGUSTUS VAN HORNE ELLIS, WHO HAD BEEN A GOLD PROSPECTOR, A SAILOR, AND A FIREMAN BEFORE BECOMING A NEW YORK LAWYER. HIS MEN SAID HE CURSED IN "TERRIBLE BURST."

WHEN THE 4TH NEW YORK BATTERY RAN OUT OF CANISTER ...

GIVE THEM SHELL! GIVE THEM SOLID SHOT! DAMN THEM, GIVE THEM ANYTHING!

BUT THE REBELS POURED IN ...

FOR GOD'S SAKE, MEN, DON'T LET THEM TAKE MY GUNS AWAY FROM ME!

COLONEL ELLIS MOUNTED A COUNTERCHARGE ...

... BUT WAS KILLED INSTANTLY WITH A BULLET THROUGH HIS HEAD.

AS OATES ADVANCED UP THE SOUTHERN SIDE OF THE LITTLE ROUND TOP...

... MEN ROSE UP FROM A ROUGHLY PILED ROCK WALL NOT 50 STEPS ABOVE THEM.

THESE MEN WERE THE 20TH MAINE, AND THEY HAD BEEN IN POSITION FOR LESS THAN 10 MINUTES.

THE WARNING OF CHIEF ENGINEER WARREN HAD NOT FALLEN ON DEAF EARS. THE BRIGADE OF COL. STRONG VINCENT WAS RUSHED INTO POSITION.

VINCENT PLACED THE 20TH MAINE ON THE SOUTHERN-MOST POSITION. HE TOLD HIS COMMANDER, COL. JOSHUA LAWRENCE CHAMBERLAIN:

THIS IS THE LEFT OF THE UNION LINE ...

... YOU UNDERSTAND. YOU ARE TO HOLD THIS GROUND AT ALL COST.

LAW'S ALABAMIANS AND TEXANS POUNDED AGAINST THE DEFENDERS OF THE LITTLE ROUND TOP. IT SEEMED AS THOUGH EVERY MAN THERE KNEW WHAT WAS AT STAKE.

THE 20TH MAINE HELD OFF ATTACK AFTER ATTACK OF THE 15TH AND 47TH ALABAMA.

FINALLY, WITH MANY MEN DEAD AND WOUNDED AND ALMOST OUT OF AMMUNITION, COLONEL CHAMBERLAIN MADE A DECISION.

FIX BAYONETS, MEN!

CHARGE!

THE MAINE MEN CAME OUT FROM BEHIND THE BOULDERS AND TREES AND FLOODED DOWN THE HILL AGAINST THE ALABAMIANS.

OATES'S MEN STUMBLED TO A HALT AND BRACED THEMSELVES.

SUDDENLY, THEY WERE GETTING FIRE FROM THEIR REAR. THE 2ND U.S. SHARPSHOOTERS THEY HAD FACED ON THE BIG ROUND TOP WERE BACK IN THE FIGHT.

THE 15TH ALABAMA HAD HAD ENOUGH. THEY BROKE AND RAN. THE 20TH MAINE, AT THE COST OF 130 OF ITS 386 MEN, HAD HELD THE FAR LEFT FLANK OF THE ARMY OF THE POTOMAC.

ON THE RIGHT OF THE LINE ON THE LITTLE ROUND TOP, THE 4TH AND 5TH TEXAS WERE HAMMERING AWAY AT STRONG VINCENT'S BRIGADE. WHEN VINCENT HIMSELF FELL, MORTALLY WOUNDED, THE 16TH MICHIGAN SEEMED ON THE BRINK OF CRUMBLING.

BUT CHIEF ENGINEER WARREN HAD NOT GIVEN UP ON THE LITTLE ROUND TOP. HE HAD MANAGED TO MANHANDLE BATTERY D, 5TH U.S. ARTILLERY ON THE SUMMIT OF THE HILL.

HE ALSO BROUGHT THE 140TH NEW YORK, WHO CAME UP TO THE SUMMIT AND CHARGED RIGHT DOWN AGAINST THE 4TH TEXAS.

THE EMERGENCY AT THE LITTLE ROUND TOP WAS OVER, BUT FARTHER NORTH, A DESPERATE FIGHT FOR WHEAT FIELDS AND PEACH ORCHARDS WAS ABOUT TO BEGIN.

WHEATFIELD & PEACH ORCHARD

ROBERT E. LEE'S PLAN TO UNLEASH A SERIES OF MEASURED HAMMER BLOWS UP THE EMMITSBURG ROAD HAD NOT DEVELOPED AS PLANNED. A PRIMARY REASON FOR THIS WAS THAT THE CONFEDERATES HAD TO MOVE GREAT DISTANCES TO KEEP UNITS UNSEEN AND UNDETECTED.

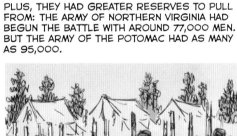

BUT BECAUSE OF THEIR ADVANTAGE OF INSIDE, INTERIOR LINES, THE UNION FORCES COULD MOVE THEIR UNITS FROM ONE CORNER OF THE BATTLEFIELD TO THE OTHER IN LESS THAN HALF AN HOUR IF MOVING AT DOUBLE TIME.

PLUS, THEY HAD GREATER RESERVES TO PULL FROM: THE ARMY OF NORTHERN VIRGINIA HAD BEGUN THE BATTLE WITH AROUND 77,000 MEN. BUT THE ARMY OF THE POTOMAC HAD AS MANY AS 95,000.

WHILE CONFEDERATE FORCES ASSAULTED THE LITTLE ROUND TOP AND THE DEVIL'S DEN, THE BRIGADES OF GEORGE ANDERSON AND HENRY BENNING FROM GEORGIA HAD BEEN BANGING AGAINST THE UNION LINE.

ANDERSON'S MEN, ALTHOUGH VETERAN ASSAULT TROOPS, HAD NOT BEEN ABLE TO CRACK THE LINE, WHICH WOULD HAVE GOTTEN THEM BEHIND SICKLES'S FLANK. THEY NEEDED HELP.

AND HELP WAS COMING. LONGSTREET WAS GETTING READY TO RELEASE MCLAWS'S DIVISION, BUT HE WAS WAITING FOR THE FULL FURY OF HOOD'S DIVISION TO SUBSIDE.

AT ABOUT 5:00 PM, LONGSTREET WALKED BRIG. GEN. JOSEPH B. KERSHAW, A SOUTH CAROLINA LAWYER WHO SEEMED BORN TO FIGHT, TO THE EMMITSBURG ROAD. HE SENT KERSHAW AND HIS MEN FORWARD WITH A SHOUT AND A WAVE OF HIS HAT.

THREE OF KERSHAW'S REGIMENTS TURNED NORTH INTO A PEACH ORCHARD.

THE OTHER 2 MOVED EAST, JOINING THE CONFEDERATE FORCES THERE TRYING TO BREAK THE UNION LINE IN A WHEAT FIELD.

AS THE 3RD AND 7TH SOUTH CAROLINA REGIMENTS PASSED THROUGH THE GEORGE RODE FARM THEY WERE RAKED BY CANISTER FIRE FROM BATTERIES ON THE WHEAT FIELD ROAD.

FACING KERSHAW'S AND ANDERSON'S BRIGADES IN THE WHEAT FIELD WAS A MIXTURE OF 3 BRIGADES FROM 2 DIFFERENT CORPS.

ONE OF THE UNION BRIGADES WAS COMMANDED BY FRENCH LAWYER, POET, AND AUTHOR PHILIPPE REGIS DENIS DE TROBRIAND, WHO RODE BEHIND HIS MEN URGING THEM ON IN A HEAVY FRENCH ACCENT.

FEDERAL TROOPS FROM 62-YEAR-OLD JAMES BARNES'S DIVISION WERE FIRING FROM BEHIND A STONE WALL, AND THEY FELT THEY COULD HOLD AGAINST "CONSIDERABLE ODDS 'TILL THE COWS COME HOME."

BUT SUDDENLY BARNES GAVE THE ORDER TO WITHDRAW!

BECAUSE OF THIS ORDER, A HUGE GAP IN THE UNION LINES OPENED UP, AND CONFEDERATE TROOPS CAME POURING THROUGH THE WHEAT FIELD.

DE TROBRIAND WAS FORCED TO FALL BACK, HIS TROOPS TAKING HEAVY CASUALTIES.

THE BRIGADES OF WILLIAM TILTON AND JACOB B. SWEITZER WERE ALSO BEING PUSHED BACK.

IN RESPONSE, HANCOCK SENT IN THE DIVISION OF BRIG. GEN. JOHN C. CALDWELL.

BEFORE MOVING UP, CALDWELL'S 2ND BRIGADE, THE FAMED IRISH BRIGADE OF PATRICK KELLY, KNELT BEFORE ITS CHAPLAIN, FATHER WILLIAM CORBY, TO RECEIVE ABSOLUTION.

AS THE SWEITZER LINE FELL APART, THE 4TH MICHIGAN REGIMENT WAS OVERRUN BY GRAY-CLAD TROOPS. THEIR COLONEL, HARRISON H. JEFFORDS, WAS TRYING TO PULL HIS UNIT BACK TO SAFETY WHEN HE SAW THE REGIMENTAL BANNER BEING TAKEN BY A REBEL SOLDIER.

JEFFORDS KILLED THE MAN WITH HIS SWORD AND TOOK THE COLORS ...

... THEN HE WAS BAYONETED THROUGH THE CHEST.

A GROUP OF OFFICERS AND MEN RUSHED TO JEFFORDS'S AID. LT. MICHAEL VREELAND KILLED THE MAN WHO HAD GOTTEN JEFFORDS, BUT HE WAS SOON SHOT AND CLUBBED. THE FLAG WAS SAVED, BUT NOT BEFORE 39 MEN FROM THE 4TH MICHIGAN WENT DOWN.

CALDWELL PUSHED HIS BRIGADES INTO THE WHEAT FIELD AS THEY REACHED IT. FIRST WAS THE BRIGADE WAS OF OLD INDIAN FIGHTER, EDWARD E. CROSS, WHO WAS MORTALLY WOUNDED NOT LONG AFTER THEY MET THE ENEMY.

NEXT CAME THE BRIGADE OF SAMUEL K. ZOOK, WHO ALSO WAS MORTALLY WOUNDED WITH A BULLET IN THE STOMACH.

THEN CAME THE IRISH BRIGADE—AND THEN THE BRIGADE OF JOHN BROOKE. THE LINES MOVED BACK AND FORTH ACROSS THE WHEAT FIELD 6 TIMES. FINALLY, THE LINE WAS RESTORED BETWEEN THE WHEAT FIELD AND THE DEVIL'S DEN.

ON MCLAWS'S LEFT WING WAS THE BRIGADE OF MISSISSIPPI CONGRESSMAN WILLIAM BARKSDALE. HIS 4 MISSISSIPPI REGIMENTS HAD BEEN GIVEN THE JOB OF ATTACKING INTO THE PEACH ORCHARD WHERE SICKLES HAD ADVANCED HIS CORPS.

A UNION BATTERY IN THE PEACH ORCHARD WAS POUNDING AWAY AT BARKSDALE'S WAITING MEN.

LONGSTREET WAITED UNTIL THE FEDERAL FORCES IN THE WHEAT FIELD WERE TOO ENGAGED TO COME TO SICKLES'S AID.

AT 6:30 PM, THE 1,600 MEN OF BARKSDALE'S BRIGADE CAME SPRINTING OUT OF THE WOODS, EACH THROAT SCREAMING THE REBEL YELL. THEY DIDN'T FIRE A SHOT BUT WERE RUNNING FLAT OUT TOWARD THEIR GOAL.

THE REBEL YELL WAS A BATTLE CRY USED BY CONFEDERATE SOLDIERS. IT HAS BEEN DESCRIBED AS A FOX HUNT *YOP YIP YIP*, A *WA-WOO-WOOHOOH*, OR A SIMPLE *YEE-HAW*. IT HAS ALSO BEEN DESCRIBED AS SIMILAR TO THE CRIES OF THE NATIVE AMERICANS.

THEY SMASHED THROUGH 2 RAIL FENCES, ALMOST AS IF THEY WEREN'T THERE. THEY WERE THROUGH THE FEDERAL LINE IN THE PEACH ORCHARD IN NO TIME.

THE 57TH AND 114TH (ZOUAVES) PENNSYLVANIA REGIMENTS PUSHED FORWARD TO COVER THE WITHDRAWAL OF SEVERAL BATTERIES BUT WERE CUT TO PIECES BY CONFEDERATE FIRE IN FRONT OF THE SHERFY FARMHOUSE.

THE 9TH MASSACHUSETTS BATTERY EXTRACTED THEMSELVES. THEY HARNESSED THE LIMBERS AND GUNS TO THE HORSES AND PULLED THE BATTERIES BACK, FIRING AS THEY WENT.

GENERAL SICKLES WAS ON HIS HORSE NEAR THE TROSTLE FARM WHEN A SOLID SHOT TOOK OFF HIS RIGHT LEG. A DRUMMER BOY TIED A TOURNIQUET AND THEN HELPED CARRY HIM FROM THE FIELD.

SICKLES WAS SEEN SITTING UP ON THE STRETCHER, PUFFING ON A BIG CIGAR.

THE III CORPS LINE WAS FALLING APART. THE BRIGADE OF CHARLES GRAHAM WAS BROKEN AND IN ROUT.

THIS OPENED UP THE SOUTHERN FLANK OF THE CORPS. THE BRIGADES OF KERSHAW AND THE NEWLY COMMITTED WOFFORD TOOK IMMEDIATE ADVANTAGE.

BRIG. GEN. ANDREW A. HUMPHREYS HAD PREPARED HIS MIND AND HIS DIVISION FOR JUST SUCH AN EMERGENCY...

HE HAD NOT LIKED THE POSITION THAT SICKLES HAD PUT THEM IN, SO HE HAD FORESEEN SUCH A SITUATION. HUMPHREYS KEPT HIMSELF FOCUSED AND UNDER CONTROL.

HE RODE BACK AND FORTH IN FRONT OF HIS MEN, KEEPING THE LINE STRAIGHT AND DIRECTING THEIR FIRE. HIS HORSE WAS SHOT 7 TIMES BEFORE IT WENT DOWN. WHEN IT DID, HE TOOK THE HORSE OF AN AIDE, ALL THE TIME TALKING TO AND CALMING HIS MEN.

BARKSDALE, STILL PUSHING HIS BRIGADE FORWARD...

...WAS FINALLY SHOT FROM THE SADDLE, HIS BODY RIDDLED WITH BULLETS.

BY NOW, NOT ONLY BARKSDALE, BUT BARKSDALE'S BRIGADE WAS FINISHED. THEY BEGAN TO SLOW AND FINALLY FALL BACK, LIKE A WAVE SLIPPING BACK INTO THE OCEAN.

A. P. HILL'S CORPS WAS NOW ON LONGSTREET'S LEFT. HILL COMMITTED THE BRIGADES OF CADMUS M. WILCOX AND DAVID LANG IN THE ADVANCE.

WINFIELD SCOTT HANCOCK SAW THEM HEADING FOR A GAP IN CEMETERY RIDGE THAT HAD BEEN LEFT THERE WHEN CALDWELL'S DIVISION WAS SENT DOWN TO THE WHEAT FIELD.

HANCOCK SENT WORD FOR JOHN GIBBON AND ALEXANDER HAYS TO SEND HELP FROM THEIR DIVISIONS TO PLUG THE HOLE...

...BUT THAT WOULD TAKE 5 MINUTES. HE NEEDED TO GAIN 5 MINUTES!

HANCOCK RODE OVER TO A SMALL UNIT OF 262 MEN STANDING IN BATTLE LINE BEHIND A BATTERY ON CEMETERY RIDGE.

WHAT REGIMENT IS THIS?

THIS IS THE 1ST MINNESOTA, GENERAL.

THEN HANCOCK SAID IN WORDS LOUD ENOUGH FOR EVERY MAN TO HEAR...

HANCOCK COULD TELL FROM THE EXPRESSIONS ON THE FACES OF THE MEN THAT THEY UNDERSTOOD WHAT THE ORDER MEANT.

THE 1ST MINNESOTA MARCHED DOWN THE HILL WITH THEIR RIFLES SHOULDERED. WITHIN 30 YARDS THEY HALTED AND FIRED A VOLLEY INTO THE ADVANCING CONFEDERATES, THEIR OWN MEN FALLING HERE AND THERE.

AS 1 MAN REMEMBERED, "WE HAD NO TIME TO WEEP."

THEN COL. WILLIAM COLVILL GAVE THE ORDER.

CHARGE BAYONETS!

THE MINNESOTANS CHARGED INTO THE GRAY MASS OF THE REGIMENT'S 262 MEN. ONLY 47 WOULD SURVIVE.

BUT HANCOCK GOT HIS 5 MINUTES.

WILCOX AND LANG PUSHED ON AS BEST THEY COULD, BUT FEDERAL TROOPS WERE SOON POURING DOWN ON THEM. FINALLY, AT ABOUT 8:00 PM, THE CONFEDERATE WAVE BEGAN TO FALL BACK.

ON THE NORTHERN END OF THE BATTLEFIELD, RICHARD EWELL'S CORPS HAD BEEN GIVEN THE JOB OF "DEMONSTRATING" BEFORE CEMETERY HILL AND CULP'S HILL SO THE FEDERAL FORCES OF HOWARD'S XII CORPS AND SLOCUM'S XII CORPS WOULD GO TO THE AID OF FORCES ATTACKED BY LONGSTREET.

HE CONFEDERATES WAITED FOR THE SOUND OF THE GUNS, BUT PERHAPS ROM SOME UNUSUAL ATMOSPHERIC CONDITION, THEY NEVER HEARD THEM.

BUT EWELL DID BEGIN AN ARTILLERY BARRAGE, WHICH DID LITTLE AGAINST THE WELL DUG-IN BRIGADE OF BRIG. GEN. GEORGE S. GREENE, A 62-YEAR-OLD ENGINEER AND WEST POINT GRADUATE.

FINALLY, AT ABOUT 8:00 PM, WITH THE LIGHT STARTING TO FADE, EWELL SENT EDWARD JOHNSON'S DIVISION OF 5,000 MEN AGAINST CULP'S HILL.

BY THEN, GREENE WAS DOWN TO 1,310 FEDERALS, MANY OF THE TROOPS IN THE AREA HAVING BEEN PULLED AWAY TO FACE LONGSTREET. HE HAD TO ABANDON SOME OF HIS FORWARD TRENCHES.

BUT HE EXPERTLY PLACED HIS MEN FOR THE GREATEST ADVANTAGE AND THEN AWAITED THE ONSLAUGHT.

GREENE'S MEN WOULD THRO[W] BACK EVERY ASSAULT, BUT JOHNSON'S WOULD OCCUPY SOME OF THE TRENCHES THA[T] HE HAD ABANDONED. SOONE[R] OR LATER, THEY WOULD HAVE TO BE DEALT WITH.

WHEN JOHNSON MADE LITTLE PROGRESS, JUBAL EARLY SENT IN HARRY T. HAYS'S LOUISIANA "TIGERS" BRIGADE AND ISAAC AVERY'S NORTH CAROLINA BRIGADE AGAINST CEMETERY HILL.

ON THE CREST OF CEMETERY HILL, INFANTRY AND ARTILLERY FOUGHT IT OUT AT POINT-BLANK RANGE WITH THE CEMETERY GATES BEHIND THEM.

FINALLY THE CONFEDERATE SURGE ROLLED BACK.

THE SECOND DAY OF THE BATTLE WAS OVER AND THE ARMY OF THE POTOMAC HAD HELD THE LINE. GENERAL MEADE CONDUCTED A WAR COUNCIL IN HIS HEADQUARTERS IN THE LEISTER HOUSE. THEY DISCUSSED WHETHER TO HOLD THEIR GROUND, ATTACK, OR AWAIT LEE'S ATTACK.

ALL AGREED TO HOLD THEIR GROUND AND AWAIT LEE'S ATTACK. AS THE MEETING BROKE UP, MEADE TURNED TO JOHN GIBBON, WHOSE DIVISION HELD THE CENTER OF THE FEDERAL LINE.

BY MORNING, JULY 3, MEADE BEGAN TO DOUBT HIS FORECAST THAT THE CONFEDERATES WOULD ATTACK THE UNION CENTER, AND HE SUSPECTED AN ASSAULT FARTHER SOUTH NEAR THE ROUND TOPS. CONSEQUENTLY, HE MOVED MANY OF HIS FORCES THERE, LEAVING A LINE OF 5,750 INFANTRYMAN, WHO WERE SOON TO FACE A VERY DETERMINED ADVANCE BY 12,000 REBELS.

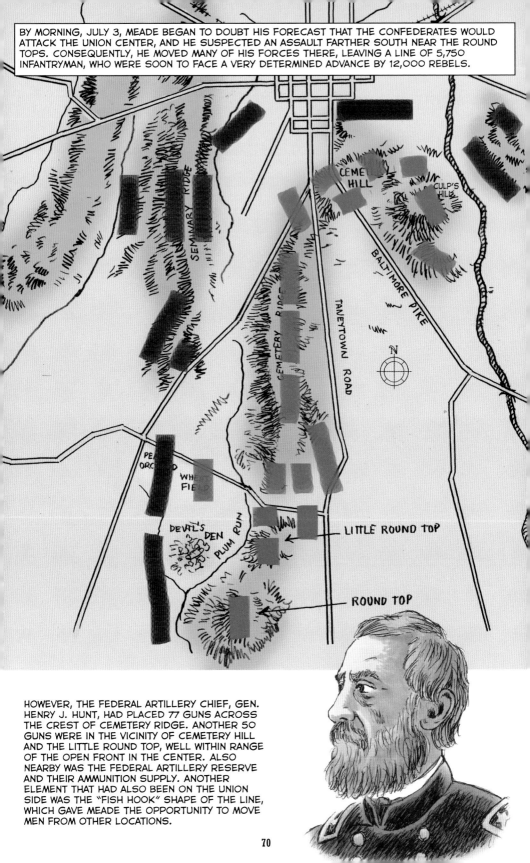

HOWEVER, THE FEDERAL ARTILLERY CHIEF, GEN. HENRY J. HUNT, HAD PLACED 77 GUNS ACROSS THE CREST OF CEMETERY RIDGE. ANOTHER 50 GUNS WERE IN THE VICINITY OF CEMETERY HILL AND THE LITTLE ROUND TOP, WELL WITHIN RANGE OF THE OPEN FRONT IN THE CENTER. ALSO NEARBY WAS THE FEDERAL ARTILLERY RESERVE AND THEIR AMMUNITION SUPPLY. ANOTHER ELEMENT THAT HAD ALSO BEEN ON THE UNION SIDE WAS THE "FISH HOOK" SHAPE OF THE LINE, WHICH GAVE MEADE THE OPPORTUNITY TO MOVE MEN FROM OTHER LOCATIONS.

THE THIRD DAY PICKETT'S CHARGE

AT THE END OF THE DAY, ROBERT E. LEE WAS CONVINCED THAT THEY HAD COME VERY CLOSE TO BREAKING THE LINE OF THE RIGHT FLANK OF THE ARMY OF THE POTOMAC. ON THAT NIGHT OF JULY 2-3, 1863, PICKETT'S DIVISION WAS ARRIVING ON THE BATTLEFIELD. LEE INTENDED TO REINFORCE PICKETT WITH TROOPS FROM A. P. HILL'S CORPS. THIS WOULD GIVE THE ASSAULT FORCE BETWEEN 12,000 AND 15,000 MEN. EWELL WOULD ATTACK AT THE SAME TIME FROM THE TRENCHES JOHNSON HAD CAPTURED THE NIGHT BEFORE ON CULP'S HILL. IT WAS AT THIS POINT THAT LONGSTREET SUGGESTED THAT THEY DISENGAGE, SLIP AROUND THE FEDERAL LEFT, AND TAKE UP A POSITION BETWEEN THE ARMY OF THE POTOMAC AND WASHINGTON. LEE IGNORED THE SUGGESTION.

BUT LONGSTREET INSISTED ON BEING HEARD, EVEN IF IT MEANT BEING INSUBORDINATE.

GENERAL, I HAVE BEEN A SOLDIER ALL MY LIFE. I HAVE BEEN WITH SOLDIERS ENGAGED IN FIGHTS BY COUPLES, BY SQUADS, COMPANIES, REGIMENTS, DIVISIONS, AND ARMIES, AND SHOULD KNOW AS WELL AS ANYONE WHAT SOLDIERS CAN DO...

...IT IS MY OPINION THAT NO 15,000 MEN EVER ARRAYED FOR BATTLE CAN TAKE THAT POSITION.

BUT DAWN BEGAN TO CREEP OVER THE BATTLEFIELD. PICKETT'S DIVISION APPROACHED ITS ASSIGNED POSITION. THE SOUND OF BATTLE WAS HEARD FROM THE NORTH.

IN THE EARLY MORNING HOURS OF JULY 3, XII HAD BEEN SENT BACK TO THE NORTHERN LINE WITH ORDERS TO RECAPTURE THE TRENCHES CAPTURED BY JOHNSON THE NIGHT BEFORE ON CULP'S HILL.

TO SUPPORT THIS ATTACK, 20 GUNS HAD BEEN BROUGHT IN, AND AT 4:30 AM THEY BEGAN THEIR BOMBARDMENT.

DURING THE NIGHT, JOHNSON HAD BEEN REINFORCED WITH 4 BRIGADES, INCLUDING THE STONEWALL BRIGADE.

THE STONEWALL BRIGADE WAS MADE UP OF THE 2ND, 4TH, 5TH, 27TH, AND 33RD VIRGINIA REGIMENTS. IT HAD BEEN COMMANDED BY STONEWALL JACKSON EARLY IN THE WAR. AT GETTYSBURG, IT WAS COMMANDED BY BRIG. GEN. JAMES A. WALKER.

JOHNSON'S BRIGADES COULD NOT STAY WHERE THEY WERE, UNDER THE ARTILLERY FIRE FROM THE BALTIMORE PIKE, BUT THEY WOULD NOT WITHDRAW. SO AT 8:00 AM THEY ATTACKED.

FOR THE NEXT 3 HOURS, THE CONFEDERATES THREW THEMSELVES AGAINST THE FEDERAL BREASTWORK. THESE ATTACKS WERE DOOMED, WHICH ANY OF THE DEFENDERS COULD CLEARLY HAVE PREDICTED FROM THE BEGINNING. BUT THE REBELS KEPT TRYING.

THE SMALL 400-MAN 1ST MARYLAND BATTALION LOST MORE THAN HALF ITS MEN, INCLUDING ITS MASCOT...

A SMALL MONGREL DOG.

73

AT 11:00 AM, THE FEDERAL FORCES ON CULP'S HILL SWEPT DOWN ON THE CONFEDERATE LEFT.

IT BECAME CLEAR TO THE REBEL COMMANDERS THAT THEY COULD NOT WITHSTAND THE FIRE FROM ABOVE AND THEY ORDERED A WITHDRAWAL.

MANY REALIZED THAT EVEN RETREAT WAS TOO DANGEROUS, AND THEY SIMPLY WAITED TO BE CAPTURED.

CULP'S HILL WOULD REMAIN IN UNION CONTROL AND EWELL'S PART IN THE BATTLE OF GETTYSBURG WAS OVER. IF HE HAD CAPTURED THE HILL ON THE FIRST DAY OF BATTLE, THE RESULTS MAY HAVE BEEN DIFFERENT—BUT THAT IS JUST SPECULATION NOW.

MEANWHILE, A 1/2 MILE WEST, 27-YEAR-OLD COL. E. PORTER ALEXANDER WAS PLACED IN CHARGE OF 140 CONFEDERATE GUNS THAT WERE TO BOMBARD THE CENTER OF THE UNION LINE ON CEMETERY RIDGE. HAVING PERFORMED WELL AT FREDERICKSBURG AND CHANCELLORSVILLE, ALEXANDER WAS BEING PLACED IN A SITUATION THAT HE WAS UNCOMFORTABLE WITH.

GENERAL LONGSTREET EXPECTED ALEXANDER TO MAKE A REPORT AFTER THE BOMBARDMENT HAD BEEN UNDER WAY FOR SOME TIME AS TO WHETHER IT HAD BEEN EFFECTIVE ENOUGH FOR THE ATTACK TO PROCEED. LONGSTREET WANTED THE ARTILLERYMAN TO DETERMINE IF THE "ARTILLERY HAD THE DESIRED EFFECT OF DRIVING THE ENEMY" OFF THE RIDGE.

ALEXANDER PROTESTED THAT THE DECISION TO ATTACK SHOULD BE MADE BEFORE THE BOMBARDMENT BEGAN.

THE ASSAULT TROOPS MOVED UP THROUGH THE WOODS BEHIND ALEXANDER'S GUNS. MANY OF THE TROOPS WERE FRESH, LIKE PICKETT'S MEN, NOT HAVING TAKEN PART IN THE FIGHTING IN THE LAST 2 DAYS.

ALEXANDER LATER WROTE, "IT IS MADNESS TO UNDERTAKE AN ADVANCE OVER OPEN GROUND AGAINST THE CENTER OF THAT LINE."

BUT MANY HAD ALREADY SEEN HEAVY BATTLE AT GETTYSBURG. LEE NOTICED SEVERAL MEN, BANDAGED FROM PREVIOUS FIGHTING. THE MEN HE SAW MAY HAVE BEEN FROM THE 26TH NORTH CAROLINA, WHICH HAD SUFFERED HEAVILY THE FIRST DAY.

MANY OF THESE POOR BOYS SHOULD GO TO THE REAR; THEY ARE NOT FIT FOR DUTY.

BUT LEE JUST RODE AWAY ON TRAVELLER, SPEAKING JUST LOUD ENOUGH TO BE HEARD:

LEE MET WITH HIS COMMANDERS WHO WOULD MAKE THE ASSAULT. HE POINTED OUT A CLUMP OF TREES IN THE CENTER OF THE LINE ON CEMETERY RIDGE. THAT WOULD BE THE POINT THAT THE ATTACKERS WERE AIMING FOR.

THE ATTACK MUST SUCCEED.

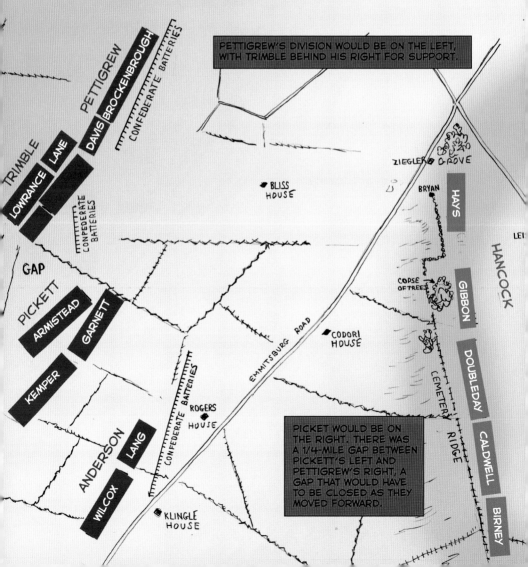

PETTIGREW'S DIVISION WOULD BE ON THE LEFT, WITH TRIMBLE BEHIND HIS RIGHT FOR SUPPORT.

PICKET WOULD BE ON THE RIGHT. THERE WAS A 1/4-MILE GAP BETWEEN PICKETT'S LEFT AND PETTIGREW'S RIGHT, A GAP THAT WOULD HAVE TO BE CLOSED AS THEY MOVED FORWARD.

SUDDENLY, AT 1:00 PM, LIKE THE FULL NOTES OF AN ORGAN IN A CHURCH, THE CANNONS OPENED UP, BEGINNING THE LARGEST ARTILLERY ENGAGEMENT OF THE WAR THUS FAR.

ON CEMETERY RIDGE, THE 5,750 FEDERAL INFANTRYMEN AND GUNNERS WHO HAD BEEN RESTING AND DOZING IN THE 90-DEGREE HEAT...

...WERE AT THAT MOMENT BROUGHT TO FULL LIFE.

SHELLS TORE INTO THE GROUND, INTO TREES, AND INTO MEN AND HORSES.

MEADE AND GIBBON WERE HAVING A MEAL OF STEW MADE "FROM AN OLD TOUGH ROOSTER" WHEN AN ORDERLY WAS TORN IN 2 BY A SHELL.

WHEN HANCOCK REALIZED THAT THE REBEL GUNS WERE TARGETING THE CLUMP OF TREES IN THE CENTER OF THE LINE, HE ORDERED ARTILLERY CHIEF HENRY HUNT TO BRING UP MORE BATTERIES.

HANCOCK FELT THAT STRONGLY RETURNING ARTILLERY FIRE WOULD ENCOURAGE THOSE UNDER THE BOMBARDMENT ON CEMETERY RIDGE.

ACTUALLY, THOSE BEHIND THE STONE, MOSTLY MEN FROM ALEXANDER WEBB'S PENNSYLVANIA BRIGADE, SOON DISCOVERED THAT MOST OF THE SHELLS WERE PASSING OVERHEAD. BECAUSE OF THE THICK WHITE SMOKE THAT THESE GUNS MADE, THE CONFEDERATES COULD NOT TELL THAT THEY WERE FIRING HIGH. MEN DISCOVERED THAT IF YOU WERE UNDER 4 FEET, YOU WERE PRETTY SAFE.

HOWEVER, THE CONTINUOUS FIRE WAS DEAFENING.

HUNT WANTED TO SLOW THEIR FIRE AND CONSERVE AMMUNITION FOR WHEN THE CONFEDERATE INFANTRY BEGIN THEIR ADVANCE.

SO HE ORDERED THE GUNS ON CEMETERY RIDGE TO HOLD THEIR FIRE AND ONLY THE GUNS ON CEMETERY HILL AND THE LITTLE ROUND TOP TO CONTINUE THEIR FIRE.

DURING THE BOMBARDMENT OF CEMETERY RIDGE,
HANCOCK RODE UPRIGHT ON HIS HORSE FOLLOWED BY
A SINGLE ORDERLY CARRYING THE CORPS FLAG.

GENERAL, THE CORPS COMMANDER OUGHT NOT TO RISK HIS LIFE THAT WAY.

THERE ARE TIMES WHEN A CORPS COMMANDER'S LIFE DOES NOT COUNT.

ALTHOUGH MOST OF THE MEN HUDDLED BEHIND THE STONE WERE SAFE, THE TROOPS ON THE FAR
SIDE, BETWEEN THE TANEYTOWN ROAD OR THE BALTIMORE PIKE, WERE NOT. THE SHELLS LANDED OR
BURST AMONG THE SUPPLY WAGONS AND THE MEDICAL FACILITIES. HORSES LAY DEAD OR MANGLED
EVERYWHERE, OR RAN RIDERLESS AND SCREAMING. THE ARMY'S AMMUNITION TRAIN AND ARTILLERY
RESERVE WERE QUICKLY MOVED A 1/2 MILE SOUTH.

BUT THE BATTERIES ON CEMETERY RIDGE WERE AN EASY MARK, EVEN IN ALL THE SMOKE. GUNS
WERE HIT, CAISSONS BLOWN UP, AND MEN TORN APART. THIS TERRIFYING SCENE WAS EVEN MORE
MAGNIFIED BY THE CRIES OF A DEVOUT YOUNG MAN NAMED ALFRED GARDNER, WHO HAD HIS ARM
BLOWN OFF.

GLORY TO GOD! I AM HAPPY! HALLELUJAH!

AT ABOUT 2:30 PM, MAJ. THOMAS W. OSBORN APPROACHED ARTILLERY CHIEF HUNT.

DOES MEADE CONSIDER AN ATTACK OF THE ENEMY DESIRABLE?

HE EXPRESSED A FERVENT HOPE THAT HE WOULD.

SHOULD WE CEASE FIRE AT ONCE, THE ENEMY COULD REACH BUT ONE CONCLUSION, THAT OF OUR BEING DRIVEN FROM THE HILL.

HUNT BEGAN TO WITHDRAW THE BATTERIES THAT WERE NEARLY OUT OF AMMUNITION OR HAD BEEN BADLY DAMAGED OR HAD CREWS THAT WERE DEPLETED. HE BROUGHT OTHER FRESH BATTERIES READY TO MOVE INTO POSITION AT ANY MOMENT.

THIS RUSE APPARENTLY WORKED, FOR BY 2:45, THE CONFEDERATE GUNS BEGAN TO FALL SILENT. OSBORN SAID THAT "A SINGULARLY DEPRESSING SILENCE" SETTLED OVER THE FIELD.

THE CONFEDERATE INFANTRY WAITING IN THE WOODS HAD ALSO GOTTEN THE WORST OF THE FEDERAL BOMBARDMENT. ABOUT 500 MEN FROM PICKETT'S DIVISION HAD BEEN KILLED OR WOUNDED.

COLONEL ALEXANDER QUICKLY SENT A MESSAGE TO PICKETT.

WHEN PICKETT GOT THIS MESSAGE, HE RODE OVER TO LONGSTREET.

"THE GUNS HAVE BEEN DRIVEN OFF. FOR GOD'S SAKE, COME QUICK, OR WE CANNOT SUPPORT YOU. AMMUNITION NEARLY OUT."

GENERAL, SHALL I ADVANCE?

CHOKED WITH EMOTION BECAUSE HE DID NOT WANT TO MAKE THIS ATTACK, LONGSTREET NEARLY NODDED.

PICKETT RODE OUT IN FRONT OF HIS MEN, WHO HAD FILED OUT OF THE WOODS AND FORMED BATTLE LINES.

CHARGE THE ENEMY, AND REMEMBER OLD VIRGINIA...

...FORWARD! GUARD CENTER! MARCH!

3 DIVISIONS OF CONFEDERATES BEGAN TO MOVE IN AN EERIE SILENCE, ORDERED NOT TO FIRE OR RAISE THE REBEL YELL. AHEAD LAY NEARLY A MILE WALK.

THE VIEW FROM THE UNION LINES
MUST HAVE BEEN INSPIRING.

BEAUTIFUL...
BEAUTIFUL.

PICKETT'S LEADING BRIGADE WAS LED BY 40-YEAR-OLD BRIG. GEN. JAMES KEMPER, A POLITICIAN
WHO HAD BEEN FIGHTING SINCE BULL RUN.

TO HIS LEFT WAS THE BRIGADE OF RICHARD
B. GARNETT, 45, RIDING A HORSE BECAUSE
OF LEG INJURY. IT WOULD MAKE HIM A
BETTER TARGET.

BEHIND HIM WAS THE BRIGADE OF 46-YEAR-
OLD LEWIS A. ARMISTEAD, AN OLD ARMY
REGULAR WHO WAS CLOSE FRIENDS OF
WINFIELD SCOTT HANCOCK.

82

ON PICKETT'S LEFT WERE BRIGADES FROM NORTH CAROLINA, TENNESSEE, MISSISSIPPI, AND ALABAMA.

COL. DENNIS O'KANE, OF THE 69TH PENNSYLVANIA, NEAR THE LITTLE COPSE OF TREES IN THE CENTER OF THE UNION LINE, TOLD HIS MEN...

HOLD YOUR FIRE UNTIL THE LAST POSSIBLE MOMENT...

...LET YOUR WORK THIS DAY BE FOR VICTORY OR DEATH.

AS PICKETT'S DIVISION LEFT THE TREES, THEY MADE A 45-DEGREE TURN TO THEIR LEFT.

WHEN THEY DID, THEY CAME UNDER THE FIRE OF GUNS ON THE LITTLE ROUND TOP AND CEMETERY RIDGE.

THE GUNS DID TERRIBLE DAMAGE, SOMETIMES TAKING 10 MEN DOWN WITH EVERY SHOT.

AS THEY NEARED THE FENCES ALONG THE EMMITSBURG ROAD, THEY SLOWED TO TAKE DOWN OR CROSS THE FENCES, AND THE GUNFIRE POURED IN ON THEM.

AND ONCE THEY HAD CROSSED, THEY STOPPED TO REFORM THEIR LINES.

ON THE UNION RIGHT, THE 8TH OHIO, UNDER THE COMMAND OF LT. COL. FRANKLIN SAWYER, HAD BEEN SENT OUT THE PREVIOUS AFTERNOON AS A SKIRMISH LINE AND HAD NEVER BEEN RECALLED.

NOW THEY OPENED FIRE ON THE CONFEDERATE LEFT THAT WAS PASSING THEM AT JUST 100 YARDS AWAY.

THE BRIGADE OF ROBERT M. MAYO CAME UNDER THEIR FIRE. ALREADY SHAKEN BY FEDERAL ARTILLERY FIRE, THE MEN HALTED AND RAN FOR THE REAR.

THE OHIOANS CHARGED INTO THEM AND TOOK 200 PRISONERS.

THIS EXPOSED THE MISSISSIPPI BRIGADE OF JOSEPH DAVIS. RESOLVE BEGAN TO CRUMBLE.

AS THE MEN OF PETTIGREW'S WING REACHED THE EMMITSBURG ROAD, THEY LINKED UP WITH PICKETT ON THE RIGHT. THEY NOW BEGAN TO GO UP THE SLIGHT RISE TO CEMETERY RIDGE.

HOME, BOYS, HOME!

REMEMBER, HOME IS OVER BEYOND THOSE HILLS!

A FEDERAL BATTERY FROM ZIEGLER'S GROVE FIRED INTO THEM.

ROUND SHOT: SIMPLE, SOLID SHOT FOR BATTERING CAVALRY AND INFANTRY IN COLUMN.

SHELL: A HOLLOW SPHERE FILLED WITH GUN POWDER, TIME-FUSED TO BURST ON IMPACT OF THE ENEMY.

SHRAPNEL: SPHERICAL CASE THAT CONTAINS MUSKET BALLS AND A CHARGE TO BURST IN THE AIR OVER THE ENEMY.

CANISTER: TIN FULL OF ROUND BALLS USED ON THE SCATTER-GUN PRINCIPLE.

GEN. ALEXANDER HAYS, WHO SEEMED TO ENJOY COMBAT, CALLED OUT TO HIS MEN:

NOW, BOYS, LOOK OUT; YOU WILL SEE SOME FUN...

FIRE!

1,700 RIFLES AND 11 CANNONS WENT OFF AT ONCE.

A GREAT MOAN FILLED THE AIR.

HAYS ORDERED HIS NORTHERN-MOST REGIMENT, THE 126TH NEW YORK, AND THE 108TH NEW YORK BATTERY, TO WHEEL SOUTH AND FIRE INTO THE REBEL RANKS.

FREDERICKSBURG! FREDERICKSBURG! FREDERICKSBURG!

THE 13TH, 14TH, AND 16TH VERMONT REGIMENTS ON THE SOUTHERN END OF THE FEDERAL LINE SAW THEIR CHANCE AND ADVANCED TO A LITTLE KNOLL TO DELIVER DEADLY FIRE INTO KEMPER'S FLANK.

GARNETT'S RIDERLESS HORSE WAS SEEN RUNNING FOR THE REAR. THE GENERAL'S BODY WAS NEVER FOUND.

STEPPING OVER THE BODIES OF THEIR COMRADES, THE MEN OF THE 14TH VIRGINIA SURGED WITHIN 10 YARDS OF THE GUNS OF THE 1ST NEW YORK BATTERY.

SEE 'EM! SEE 'EM!

FIRE!

ON THE NORTHERN ANGLE OF THE STONE WALL WERE THOSE LEFT OF THE 26TH NORTH CAROLINA WHO CROSSED OVER AND WERE THERE FOR JUST A SHORT TIME BEFORE THEY WERE PUSHED BACK.

THEY HOLD THE DISTINCTION OF SUFFERING THE HIGHEST CASUALTIES IN PICKETT'S CHARGE.

IN THE CENTER, THE CONFEDERATES WERE CROSSING THE WALL WITH LEWIS ARMISTEAD LEADING THEM.

THE 71ST PENNSYLVANIA HAD BEEN BROKEN THROUGH, BUT OTHER UNITS WERE RUSHING TO THE LINE.

COME ON, BOYS! GIVE 'EM THE COLD STEEL!

BOTH GENERALS HANCOCK AND GIBBON WERE BADLY WOUNDED, BUT BOTH WOULD SURVIVE.

THE 69TH PENNSYLVANIA, THE 19TH MASSACHUSETTS, AND THE 42ND NEW YORK RUSHED INTO THE ANGLE.

WITHIN MINUTES, EVERY CONFEDERATE WHO HAD CROSSED THE WALL WAS EITHER DEAD OR CAPTURED.

THE SOUTHERN TIDE ROLLED BACK.

GENERAL LEE RODE OUT TO MEET THE RETURNING SURVIVORS.

THERE WERE 2 CAVALRY ENGAGEMENTS LATER THAT DAY, ONE TO THE EAST AND ONE TO THE SOUTH, BUT EVERYTHING HAD ALL BEEN DECIDED.

DEFEAT & VICTORY

LINCOLN WAS OVERJOYED WITH THE VICTORY, BUT PUSHED FOR MEADE TO ATTACK LEE AND FINISH THE JOB—MAYBE EVEN FINISH THE WAR.

STILL SEEING THE GUNS POINTED AT HIM FROM SEMINARY RIDGE, MEADE WOULD NOT BE PUSHED.

HOW DO WE KNOW THAT LEE WILL NOT ATTACK ME AGAIN?

WE HAVE DONE WELL ENOUGH.

ON THE NEXT DAY, JULY 4, PATROL WENT OUT AND FOUND THAT THE CONFEDERATES HAD WITHDRAWN FROM THE TOWN OF GETTYSBURG AND FROM THE AREAS NEAR THE ROUND TOPS. BUT WHEN FEDERAL SKIRMISHERS NEARED THE EMMITSBURG ROAD, THEY GOT HEAVY FIRE FROM SEMINARY RIDGE.

THAT AFTERNOON, RAIN BEGAN TO FALL ON THE BATTLEFIELD AND THAT NIGHT THE CONFEDERATE WAGON TRAINS OF SUPPLIES AND WOUNDED BEGAN TO MOVE SOUTH.

OLD JOHN BURNS HAD BEEN CAPTURED DURING THE BATTLE, BUT WAS RELEASED WHEN THE CONFEDERATE INFANTRY FINALLY PULLED OUT.

ON JULY 5, MEADE BEGAN SLOWLY TO UPROOT THE ARMY OF THE POTOMAC AND HALFHEARTEDLY PURSUE LEE. LINCOLN WANTED MEADE TO ATTACK LEE AGAIN BEFORE HE CROSSED THE POTOMAC AND POTENTIALLY END THE WAR.

THAT SAID, MUCH OF THE ARMY WAS EXHAUSTED, AND SO WAS MEADE.

BUT MEADE ALSO KNEW THAT THE ARMY OF NORTHERN VIRGINIA WAS A DANGEROUS OPPONENT EVEN IN ITS CONDITION AFTER GETTYSBURG. MEADE DIDN'T WANT TO TAKE A CHANCE.

THEN WORD CAME FROM MISSISSIPPI THAT VICKSBURG HAD SURRENDERED ON JULY 4. A MAJOR TURNING POINT IN THE WAR HAD OCCURRED, BOTH IN THE EAST AND THE WEST.

MEANWHILE, THE PEOPLE OF GETTYSBURG HAD TO DEAL WITH THE HUGE NUMBERS OF THE DEAD AND DYING. WITHIN DAYS, PHOTOGRAPHERS ALEXANDER GARDNER AND MATHEW BRADY ARRIVED TO DOCUMENT THE BATTLEFIELDS AND THE BODIES.

NO ONE WILL KNOW FOR SURE HOW MANY DIED AT GETTYSBURG, BUT THE OFFICIAL COUNT FOR THE ARMY OF THE POTOMAC WAS 23,049 DEAD, WOUNDED, AND MISSING.

LEE'S LOSSES ARE MUCH HARDER TO DETERMINE, BUT THE TOTAL CASUALTIES ARE BELIEVED TO BE MORE THAN 28,000.

ONE NUMBER IS KNOWN FOR SURE. JENNIE WADE, A 20-YEAR-OLD CITIZEN OF GETTYSBURG, WAS THE ONLY CIVILIAN KILLED IN THE BATTLE. SHE WAS BAKING BREAD IN HER KITCHEN WHEN A BULLET PASSED THROUGH 2 DOORS AND HIT HER IN THE BACK, KILLING HER INSTANTLY.

JENNY'S FIANCEE, JACK SKELLY, HAD BEEN WOUNDED AND CAPTURED BY CONFEDERATE FORCES IN VIRGINIA. HE DIED ON JULY 12 WITHOUT KNOWING OF JENNY'S DEATH.

GETTYSBURG WAS THE GREATEST BATTLE EVER FOUGHT ON THE WESTERN HEMISPHERE AND THE TURNING POINT OF THE AMERICAN CIVIL WAR. BUT IT WAS MORE THAN THAT. IT WAS A MARK BETWEEN WHAT HAD COME BEFORE AND WHAT CAME AFTER. LINCOLN KNEW THAT HE COULD STILL LOSE THE WAR, BUT NOW HE KNEW THAT HE COULD WIN IT.

GETTYSBURG DID FOR AMERICA WHAT WATERLOO AND STALINGRAD DID FOR EUROPE. IF WINSTON CHURCHILL HAD BEEN ALIVE AT THE TIME, HE MAY HAVE REFERRED TO GETTYSBURG AS THE HINGE OF FATE.

FRANCIS BARLOW SURVIVED HIS TERRIBLE WOUND AT GETTYSBURG AND WENT ON TO THE RANK OF MAJOR GENERAL. HE BECAME ONE OF THE FOUNDERS OF THE AMERICAN BAR ASSOCIATION. JOHN B. GORDON WENT ON TO BE ONE OF LEE'S MOST TRUSTED LIEUTENANTS. HE THEN BECAME GOVERNOR OF GEORGIA AND A U.S. SENATOR. LEGEND HAS IT THAT THEY MET EACH OTHER AT A DINNER IN WASHINGTON, D.C. YEARS LATER, EACH BELIEVING THE OTHER DEAD, AND THAT THEY BECAME LIFELONG FRIENDS. EXPERTS SAY THIS NEVER HAPPENED. STILL, IT IS A BEAUTIFUL LEGEND.

GETTYSBURG LAWYER DAVID WILLS SUGGESTED TO THE PENNSYLVANIA GOVERNOR THAT A SOLDIERS' CEMETERY BE ESTABLISHED WHERE THE UNION DEAD COULD BE BURIED WITH DIGNITY AND HONOR.

BUT WHAT OF THE CONFEDERATE DEAD? WERE THEY NOT REBELS AND TRAITORS?

THE SOUTHERNERS WERE BURIED ALONG ROADS, IN DITCHES AND TRENCHES, AND IN MASS GRAVES WITH VERY LITTLE EFFORT FOR IDENTIFICATION. IN 1872, THE SOUTHERN STATES BEGAN THE DIFFICULT PROCESS OF GATHERING THE BODIES FOR REBURIAL IN SOUTHERN CEMETERIES.

ONE OF THESE BODIES WAS NO DOUBT GENERAL RICHARD B. GARNETT, WHOSE BODY WAS NEVER IDENTIFIED OR RECOVERED. YEARS LATER, HIS SWORD WAS DISCOVERED IN A BALTIMORE PAWN SHOP.

WHEN THE PHOTOGRAPH FOUND ON THE UNIDENTIFIED BODY OF AMOS HUMISTON OF THE 154TH NEW YORK WAS PUBLISHED IN NORTHERN NEWSPAPERS, THE NATION WENT WILD TO IDENTIFY HIM. A CONTEST TO WRITE A POEM ABOUT HIM WAS SET TO MUSIC AND INCLUDED THE WORDS, "O FATHER, GUARD THE SOLDIER'S WIFE / AND FOR HIS ORPHANS CARE."

IN OCTOBER, PHILINDA HUMISTON, WHO HAD NOT RECEIVED A LETTER FROM HER HUSBAND SINCE THE BATTLE, SAW THE PHOTOGRAPH IN THE *AMERICAN PRESBYTERIAN*. SHE EXPLAINED TO AUTHORITIES THAT SHE HAD MAILED THE PHOTOGRAPH TO HER HUSBAND SHORTLY BEFORE HIS DEATH.

PROCEEDS FROM SALES OF THE SHEET MUSIC WERE USED TO ESTABLISH THE NATIONAL HOMESTEAD AT GETTYSBURG, A HOME FOR SOLDIERS' ORPHANS. PHILINDA HUMISTON WAS THEIR FIRST MATRON.

ON THURSDAY, NOVEMBER 19, 1863, UP TO 20,000 PEOPLE GATHERED AROUND A PLATFORM TO WITNESS THE DEDICATION OF THE SOLDIERS' NATIONAL CEMETERY IN GETTYSBURG. 3,577 UNION SOLDIERS WERE BURIED THERE, HALF OF THEM UNKNOWN.

ONE OF THE FOREMOST SPEAKERS OF THE DAY, EDWARD EVERETT, SPOKE FOR NEARLY 2 HOURS.

THEN PRESIDENT LINCOLN AROSE TO ADD A FEW APPROPRIATE WORDS.

FOUR SCORE AND SEVEN YEARS AGO OUR
FATHERS BROUGHT FORTH ON THIS CONTINENT
A NEW NATION, CONCEIVED IN LIBERTY, AND
DEDICATED TO THE PROPOSITION THAT ALL MEN
ARE CREATED EQUAL.

NOW WE ARE ENGAGED IN A GREAT CIVIL
WAR, TESTING WHETHER THAT NATION, OR ANY
NATION, SO CONCEIVED AND SO DEDICATED,
CAN LONG ENDURE. WE ARE MET ON A GREAT
BATTLE-FIELD OF THAT WAR. WE HAVE COME
TO DEDICATE A PORTION OF THAT FIELD, AS A
FINAL RESTING PLACE FOR THOSE WHO HERE
GAVE THEIR LIVES THAT THE NATION MIGHT
LIVE. IT IS ALTOGETHER FITTING AND PROPER
THAT WE SHOULD DO THIS.

BUT, IN A LARGER SENSE, WE CAN NOT
DEDICATE, WE CAN NOT CONSECRATE, WE CAN
NOT HALLOW THIS GROUND. THE BRAVE MEN,
LIVING AND DEAD, WHO STRUGGLED HERE,
HAVE CONSECRATED IT, FAR ABOVE OUR POOR
POWER TO ADD OR DETRACT. THE WORLD WILL
LITTLE NOTE, NOR LONG REMEMBER WHAT WE
SAY HERE, BUT IT CAN NEVER FORGET WHAT
THEY DID HERE. IT IS FOR US THE LIVING,
RATHER, TO BE DEDICATED HERE TO THE
UNFINISHED WORK WHICH THEY WHO FOUGHT
HERE HAVE THUS FAR SO NOBLY ADVANCED.
IT IS RATHER FOR US TO BE HERE DEDICATED
TO THE GREAT TASK REMAINING BEFORE US—
THAT FROM THESE HONORED DEAD WE TAKE
INCREASED DEVOTION TO THAT CAUSE FOR
WHICH THEY GAVE THE LAST FULL MEASURE
OF DEVOTION—THAT WE HERE HIGHLY RESOLVE
THAT THESE DEAD SHALL NOT HAVE DIED IN
VAIN—THAT THIS NATION, UNDER GOD, SHALL
HAVE A NEW BIRTH OF FREEDOM—AND THAT
GOVERNMENT OF THE PEOPLE, BY THE PEOPLE,
FOR THE PEOPLE, SHALL NOT PERISH FROM
THE EARTH.